Hiking the Road to Ruins

DAVID A. STEINBERG

Hiking
the Road to Ruins

Day Trips and Camping Adventures to
Iron Mines,
Old Military Sites,
and Things Abandoned
in the New York City Area . . .

and Beyond

Rivergate Books, an imprint of Rutgers University Press
New Brunswick, New Jersey, and London

Library of Congress Cataloging-in-Publication Data

Steinberg, David A., 1962–
 Hiking the road to ruins : day trips and camping adventures to iron
mines, old military sites, and things abandoned in the New York City area—
and beyond / David A. Steinberg.
   p.   cm.
 ISBN-13: 978-0-8135-4035-1 (pbk. : alk. paper)
 1. Hiking—New York (State)—New York (region)—Guidebooks.
 2. Abandoned mines—New York (State)—New York (region)—Guidebooks.
 I. Title.
  GV191.42.N7S74   2007
  796.51097471—dc22
                                                              2006026825

Manufactured in the United States of America

This book is fondly dedicated to my family:

My lovely and patient wife, Emily, who supported me throughout the long research and writing phases, and my seven-year-old son, Noah, who endures horror movies and hiking to ruins with me.

My parents, Phillip and Gloria Steinberg, who taught me to love camping, hiking, the outdoors, and adventure. They taught by example that all life is sacred. Dad would never kill any stray insects that found their way into our home; he would trap them and carefully release them outside. Bravo.

Contents

Acknowledgments ix

Introduction 1
Preparation 4
Leading and Not Leading Hikes 9
Using GPS 14
1 The Army Tunnels 16
2 Beacon Mountain Casino 22
3 The Boston Harbor Islands 30
4 The C&O Canal 38
5 Camp Hero 47
6 The Cornish Estate 61
7 Cranberry Lake Preserve 66
8 Dennytown Mines 73
9 Doodletown 79
10 Dunderburg Spiral Railway 87
11 Great Camp Santanoni 92
12 Hasenclever Iron Trail 99
13 Island Pond Ranger Cabin 108
14 Mines! All Mines! 112
15 Mount Hope Historical Park 119
16 Open Adits 124
17 Overlook Mountain House 132
18 The Pergola 136
19 Ramapo Valley County Reservation 143
20 The Roomy Mine 149
21 Southford Falls State Park 156
22 Watchung Reservation 160
23 West Point Foundry 171

Appendix 175

Acknowledgments

Raymond Lech, book editor extraordinaire.

Shelley Fyman for early edits and writing advice.

Thumbs up to the intrepid Road to Ruins Investigation Team, primarily Todd Rutt but also Marcus Lieberman and my son, Noah, who freely and of their own will (except in Noah's case) spent many days and weekends with me, hiking and camping in some odd places.

Dave Rabin and Outdoor Singles in Queens, New York.

Jonathan Scherer for free legal advice.

A solemn nod is given to the memories of Douglas Legg and Gregg Sanders, whose sad stories are recounted herein.

To the way-underground IMF Photo Team: how does the sunlight feel?

David Lynch of Intelics.com for creating and administering the RTR web site.

And finally: Murray Scherer, we all miss you.

Maps and photos are by the author unless otherwise indicated.

Hiking the Road to Ruins

Introduction

It isn't about the trees.

Don't get me wrong, because getting into the woods for a day is one of my favorite things to do. No matter how my body might ache, how distracted I might be with home or work issues, a good challenging day on the trail resets me in a way nothing else will. A long time ago, I discovered that hiking to goals is more rewarding than just ambling around a circuit, and you might get some good pictures, too.

Historical iron mining, the industrial revolution, and the explosive population growth of the New York metropolitan area have left us many opportunities for ruins discoveries in forest settings, all within close proximity of the busiest city on earth. War is also very good for ruin hunters, as one obsolete installation after another becomes legally available for exploration.

Be sure to take a lot of photos as you explore. Remote historic sites change from year to year, and rarely for the better. The old wooden buildings will eventually collapse or burn, some mine will fill in, or an old ghost town will be bulldozed. Get there while things are still standing and witness the sad magnificence of these once busy destinations.

I especially welcome fellow hike leaders of all sorts to these adventures. Even if you have never hiked a step, much less led a hike, anyone caught using this book is a de facto *hike leader*, an awesome responsibility and social promotion.

There are numerous books about western ghost towns but I have never seen a compilation on ruins or ghosts in the New York City area. Within a relatively short drive of the New York metropolitan area are a multitude of colorful abandoned sites. This book is not meant to be the last word on the subject or an exhaustively researched historical dissertation but more of a companion piece to several excellent books on hiking in the New York area:

* *New York Walk Book* and *New Jersey Walk Book* by the New York–New Jersey Trail Conference
* *Iron Mine Trails* by Edward Lenik, New York–New Jersey Trail Conference
* *Harriman Trails* by William J. Myles, New York–New Jersey Trail Conference
* *Vanishing Ironworks of the Ramapos* by James M. Ransom, Rutgers University Press

My intention is to put together a collection of good ideas for hikes and explorations, written as if you, the reader, are on one of my hikes. Ruins, iron mines, or historic shelters, for example, make especially fascinating goals for day trip adventures.

My criteria for inclusion for ruins, mines, etc. are:

* Within a two-hour drive of New York City (in most cases)
* The site is on a clearly marked trail or identifiable woods road
* Legally accessible
* Photogenic
* The hike itself is a pleasant nature experience

Special note to hike leaders: Because I've outlined the exact location of sites and listed most of the things I've come across, this book might take the thrill of discovery away from some people. For you, this is just another regrettable burden of the responsibility you'll unflinchingly shoulder as you lead your friends on hikes.

The motivation for my exploration has always been about photography. When I began seriously taking photos as a hobby, I would drag my friends all over the place in the name of good pictures. Fortunately, I know people who like to photograph as much as I do and are into the adventure. It wasn't long after that when I started leading hikes for different organizations. I began searching out interesting places to hike, for things and places that are visually stimulating and historically interesting.

I know that there is a twisted element of the population that enjoys accessing abandoned buildings, military leftovers, and the like, and not always legally. They are called Urban Explorers (they have plenty of self-congratulatory web sites) and even do this odd activity in organized groups. Urban Explorers have their own noble code of ethics: do no damage to gain access, take nothing. They are not about breaking and entering, and even less about law enforcement interface.

My affiliation with the elite IMF Photo Team, pioneers in high-concept urban exploration during the 1980s and 1990s, has previously not been known but my work with Research & Development at the IMF's New York office paved the way for me to begin chronicling the Road to Ruins. After some memorable missions the IMF became dormant as we grew up and stopped sneaking into places. Eventually the IMF was placed on inactive status, but the curiosity remained and so years later the Road to Ruins Investigation Team became a logical extension of that secret investigative group in a quest to do it legally. Many former IMF Photo Team operatives have participated in Road to Ruins investigations.

My ultimate purpose in putting this book together is to inspire the reader to action; to get you on the trail to satisfy some curiosity. I hope the information here sparks your interest in finding out more: a perfect map, a book, a source that will encourage even further exploration to discover some curious, mysterious, photogenic relic of our past.

Know a good ruin somewhere? Infiltrate www.TheRoadToRuins .com with your tips or comments.

Preparation

Items to Bring or Wear

Ankle-supportive hiking shoes, waterproof
   is a plus

Copy of the trail map, with the route
   highlighted and arrowed

FRS (Family Radio Service) two-way radios

Fully charged cell phone

GPS (Global Positioning System) receiver

Hand towel

Light-colored long pants

Sunglasses

Watch

Wicking clothing

Wide-brimmed hat

Items to Pack

Binoculars

Bug repellent

Camera and film, memory
   card, extra batteries

Compass (nonelectronic)

First aid kit

Food and water, snacks

Original trail map

Paper

Pen

Plastic supermarket bags for trash

Rainwear

Reliable flashlight (bring two if you
   know you'll be inside a mine or ruin)

Sun tan lotion

Water filter

Whistle

My First Aid Kit

Alcohol pads

Antibiotic ointment

Bandage tape

Band-Aids

Disposable lighter

Gauze

Itch relief pen (ammonia)

Moleskin (for blisters)

Pain reliever (small bottle of aspirin, acetaminophen, or ibuprofen with the cotton pressed in firmly to eliminate the rattling noise while hiking)

Pepto-Bismol tablets

Pocket knife

Rubber gloves

Sewing kit (small, for minor repairs)

Tick pliers

Triangular bandage (sling)

Speaking the Language of the Trail

Blazes are colored markings that appear on rocks and trees. They are the street signs of the trail. Each trail has its own color (or design, or combination of colors). It is not unusual to have several differently colored blazes sharing the same path. A single blaze of one color means the trail continues straight ahead in the direction you are going. Trail turns are indicated by two stacked blazes, with the top blaze to the left or right of the blaze below. The trail turns in the direction of the top blaze. A triangular configuration is the beginning or end of the trail.

A **woods road** is an old dirt or gravel road used as a trail. It may be marked or unmarked.

A **cairn** (pronounced "carn") is a conspicuous pile of rocks that serves the same purpose as a blaze. There is no correct size. In this part of New York and New Jersey they are usually placed on unmarked trails to point the way as you go. Sometimes they alert the hiker that an unmarked spur branches off to an overlook, mine, or other feature that is not on the trail proper. They are less formal than blazes and not generally placed by recognized trail maintainers.

Bushwhacking is when you leave the known path and walk through trail-less woods to get to a particular place.

Primitive campsites are typically remote tent sites. Staying at them requires survival planning.

The **New York–New Jersey Trail Conference** is the area's major recognized trail maintainer. In addition to clearing and blazing trails they print most of the hiking books and maps we use for reference and navigation, such as the *New York Walk Book*, frequently referred to as the *Walk Book*.

Abbreviations are commonly used when discussing trails. Fellow hikers you encounter on the way might ask how far down the intersection is where the AT (Appalachian Trail) crosses the LP (Long Path).

Cell Phones

Annoying? Yes. Critical to have along? Yes.

When you are the leader, your hikers should have your cell phone number keyed into their phones. This way, they can contact you if they get lost or injured (assuming service is available).

Chatting away on the trail is the height of clueless arrogance.

Safety

I do not advocate entering places that appear to be dangerous or are closed to the public, so use common sense at all times. Do not take any chances with your health or well-being and think twice before taking foolish risks. Hike with a partner when you can.

I strongly suggest that you bring your properly stocked backpack with you everywhere you go at all times when hiking, even when entering places that look safe (such as iron mines that don't appear to be very deep), or you think you'll only be in "for a minute." How stupid would you feel if you twisted an ankle and your pack (with first aid) was just out of reach, or if a rock fall prevented an exit and your pack was on the other side of it? Don't take chances by dropping your pack when your well-being might be at stake.

On these explorations you'll frequently be hiking on unmarked trails, exploring military remnants, and inspecting deep iron mines. Before you go *anywhere*, give a detailed itinerary to someone (family, a park ranger, or leave a map on your desk at home), especially mentioning whom you're with and when you expect to return. Photocopy the trail map twice and give one copy to someone at home with the intended route highlighted in yellow with arrows showing direction of travel. You can also buy an extra copy of this book, thoughtfully give it to your contact, and tell them which chapter you're following. Always check in when you return. Use the other copy of the trail map to navigate while you keep the original safe and dry in your backpack.

Keep a full change of clothing (jacket or sweatshirt, footwear, underwear, socks, shirt, and pants) in the car for your return. Extra food and water are also things that you'll be glad you stashed in the trunk. You should be prepared to deal with all sorts of surprises on these hikes.

Flashlight

A good, reliable flashlight is a beautiful thing. I like weatherproof flash-lights with wide reflectors (three inches is *very* nice) and room some-where inside for an extra bulb. When I know I'll need one for an infiltration, I'll bring one big four-cell light (spring-contact lantern bat-teries are too heavy for backpacking) with a large reflector and one two-cell (usually D-cell) as backup. Whenever I'm on the trail I rou-tinely carry the two-cell. Always test your lamp in a dark room the night before the trip.

Maglites are indeed bright, but much too heavy and the bulbs have a short burn time. I don't care much for headlamp-style lights as a primary source of illumination when exploring. The bright beam pointing down from my head obscures my vision. They are better suited to life in the campsite when backpacking. I appreciate the need for hands-free lighting, but a belt or chest-mounted light is better when nosing around in dark places.

I always use Krypton bulbs in the field because they are much brighter than standard bulbs and cost about the same. Halogen bulbs are also excellent but a good deal more expensive; some have an annoying dark spot in the center of the beam. I keep spare bulbs some-where in the flashlight if there is enough room; otherwise they go in my first aid kit. Standard bulbs are good for reading at night.

Alkaline cells are a smart choice for reliable power. They hold a charge when unused, dim much more predictably than other types of power cells (thus, you know far in advance when it's time to change cells), and never die suddenly. You can leave new alkalines in your pack over time and feel secure that they'll perform when you install them. They are more expensive than "heavy duty" or "regular" cells and are heavier than rechargeable batteries.

NiCad (nickel-cadmium) cells have a shorter burn time, an unfor-tunate recharge memory (if you recharge them before they're fully dis-charged they'll never again charge up completely), and a sharp power use down-curve, which is not necessarily a bad thing since they give almost full power output until they quit. They like to be discharged completely before recharging.

NiMH (nickel-metal hydride) cells have a comparable life to NiCads' and no recharge memory. They lose some of their charge when they aren't used, so if you use NiMHs, or bring some as extras, you must recharge them every time you go out. When they're used up, the power drops off suddenly, as with NiCads. For longer life, try to avoid discharging them completely and recharge as soon as possible.

NiCads and NiMHs are noticeably lighter to carry.

Never mix different battery types. Some devices, such as GPS, require you to set the device for the type of battery you're using.

Maps

The personally rendered, hand-drawn maps presented herein are for general location purposes only. I would not rely on them for navigation. Pick up the maps listed in the chapter introductions.

Some maps, such as those put out by the New York–New Jersey Trail Conference, are updated every few years and reflect trail relocations, new trails, and so on. They're also printed on tear-proof, waterproof paper, making them last a very long time. Don't hang onto old maps. Update often and check web sites for new information.

Research

Start from the top and work down: the National Park Service, National Forest Service, New York State Department of Environmental Conservation, or state vacation guides are great places to begin researching a trail. From there, write, call, or email the park of your choice. Park rangers are the best source for specific answers to questions about campsites or trail conditions in their jurisdiction and they can frequently tip you off to something interesting that isn't on the map. Historical societies sometime sponsor hikes to old mines or historic sites of interest. Hiking clubs (Appalachian Mountain Club, Sierra Club, etc.) are valuable resources and orienteering clubs sometimes produce excellent maps of trails. Web searches are valuable, also. Topozone.com is a great web site for downloading maps or getting GPS coordinates in UTM (Universal Transverse Mercator), although they don't always indicate hiking trails. See the chapter on using GPS for more details on UTM.

Leading and Not Leading Hikes

Not Leading

Be prepared because you are ultimately responsible for your own personal comfort and safety. Make sure you have the right gear and food, a trail map, and are behaving appropriately. If in doubt, be sure to ask questions before you go. The leader isn't your mother or father but will usually do anything possible to assure an enjoyable outing. After all, isn't that the idea?

Try to enjoy your time hiking through the peaceful green forest and over those bracing mountains. You aren't at work! Guiding people through the woods effectively isn't your problem, so let the leader lead. If you don't agree with the way things are going, rational discussion must displace anger in any debate. Questioning a decision on the leader's part is fine but just because you don't agree doesn't mean someone is wrong. Heated arguing helps no one and turns the day sour. Most seasoned hike leaders should be confident enough in their abilities not to be threatened by a reasonable question or challenge. You might learn something from another point of view.

Given that the person leading the trip knows the route and how to get back (and very possibly has the car keys), it is in your interest to protect your leader, as the troops protect their general. This sounds severe and overstated for simple day hikes, and maybe it is, but the point is that if you cut off the head, the body dies.

Leading a Hike

When you imperiously set yourself up as a "hike leader," you pick the destination and research the history or natural features of the hike, secure the map, and make some copies for your friends, who may or may not know how to read it properly. You make sure your hikers are properly outfitted, decide how to get to the trailhead, select the trails you'll need to take, lead your hikers on the trail, find everything, assume responsibility for first aid, hope that the destination you've selected is worth the time investment (but you're in the woods, so how bad can it be, anyway?), and get them out safely, all the while enjoying the day. You must be strong and resourceful . . . leading a successful hike isn't simple.

There is an assumption on the part of your hikers that you know what you're doing. Here's your opportunity to look like a genius by leading a hike that goes well and then enjoy all the gushing applause and cheers at the end. Unfortunately, you also open yourself up to criticism and disappointment when things don't go as planned. The margin of difference between a rousing success and a substandard failure can be slim.

Some quasi-military aphorisms become altogether fitting and proper:

- A plan is subject to change in the field.
- Hope for the best and prepare for the worst.
- Pressure makes diamonds.
- Good luck is the result of good planning. (I got that one from a fortune cookie.)

The underlying principle of all this is that it is important to plan ahead and have a reasonable strategy for the day's explorations. You'll need to be "liquid" and make changes as needed. Impossible water crossings or path-obstructing hazards might require you to alter the line of attack. Learn from your mistakes.

Putting your feet on the trail is the easy part of leading, but it's the people management aspects that are the real challenge! Be decisive. Waffling = indecision = weakness = your hikers won't trust you. Stick with the plan. "Firm but fair" is my guideline when leading groups. If you are the leader, it doesn't mean you are the sole decision-maker. As with the president, your hikers are your cabinet and you need to listen to them, but ultimate responsibility for the course of action is yours. You're the leader! Remember that if someone gets lost or hurt; it will be up to you to get them to safety.

When leading a hike for a group, and assuming you are not being paid to perform these duties, you have a responsibility to protect those who have entrusted themselves to you. If you're getting paid, you also have a legal responsibility to supply the service you've been contracted to provide.

Some rules of thumb that may be helpful on the trail:

1 Count noses before the hike begins. Assign informal "buddies" or let participants pick their own. Do a head count at every rest stop.

2 Inform your hikers that if they lose the group they should remain on the trail and stay put: soon enough, the leader will learn that someone is not there and will backtrack in an attempt to find that person. If the lost hiker has moved off the original route, the problems really begin.

3 Participants may hike at their own pace but instruct them to always wait at any trail intersections, including those at unmarked trails or woods roads. They probably don't know the route you're taking that day, so they must stop. This also allows the group to come together and some folks can rest while the others catch up.

4 Have your hikers inform you if they are feeling any pain at all. Meds in your first aid kit should be able to cope with anything from headaches and indigestion to forming blisters. You can only move as fast as your slowest hiker.

5 Hikers must notify you or their buddy when they are leaving the trail for bathroom breaks. Some clubs have informally scheduled "separations" where the men and the ladies split off.

6 FRS two-way transceivers are a good thing. Pick at least a 5-mile set, and once you appoint a "sweep" (the last person to follow the group on the hike) give them the other radio and stay in touch. Make sure you get your radio back after the hike! Put your name and phone number on it somewhere.

7 Three of anything (fires, shirts), usually in a triangular configuration, is the international distress signal. The SOS is antiquated. If you are attempting to signal with your flashlight, patterns of three dots with a suitable pause between each set is standard.

8 Enthusiasm is contagious. If you're enjoying yourself and having fun, your group will pick up on it. Your hike will be a success, no matter what. If you're having a lousy day and wish you were home watching the Mets game, they'll pick up on that, too.

9 Respect the environment you're hiking through. Be sure your hikers do no damage, don't litter, don't trespass on private property, or throw rocks from high points because someone might be hiking below you.

Emergency Measures

Red Cross First Aid Basics and CPR certifications are good things to have before you begin hiking or leading groups. Another good thing to have ready is a strategy for when things go wrong.

Keep a cool head. If someone has a serious injury but it does not prevent them from hiking, get to civilization/a road/ranger station/a home ASAP. This is not always possible, of course. The important thing is to stay in control and be reassuring to your charge. Keep encouraging them to move, no matter what, because they will still be in pain whether they get help quickly or not. They need to know that everyone will fare better if they keep moving towards proper medical care. Attempt to make a cell phone call to 911 and see if you can tell them where you expect to emerge from the woods.

A far more critical situation is when the injury prevents the victim from walking. Not even a broken leg or sprained ankle will prevent someone who is properly motivated from getting out of the woods but an unconscious person isn't going anywhere and carrying someone out is rarely the smart thing to do in that circumstance. Moving a wounded person is the last thing to be attempted and could make their injury worse. Furthermore, it will slow down the move towards help if you're dragging an injured person along. You might have to leave them there while you get help. It's a tough judgment call on the leader's part.

Make your injured hiker as comfortable as possible; mark his position on your map or with your GPS and then get help, possibly bringing someone with you. Have others stay with the injured person. Do *not* send someone else with your map while you stay with the injured. As the leader, you alone know exactly where your hiker is and you minimize the risk that your rescuer will get lost while frantically running through the woods.

It might be smart to drop your heavy pack (but always carry water and a map with you) and move out as quickly as possible. This way, others can use your first aid kit, food, extra water, and clothing to comfort the victim. They might want to build a fire for warmth and signal purposes. If you have a cell phone with good reception, just make the call and stay with the injured until assistance arrives.

If it's just the two of you, leave the injured and get help as quickly as possible if there is no cell service available.

Getting Lost

We all miss an intersection, bear left when the trail goes right, or lose the blaze. When it happens, maintain your grace under fire. Don't try to fix things by bushwhacking to where you think the trail is but turn around and backtrack to the last blaze.

Once you are back at the last blaze, look around. In most cases, you should be able to see the next blaze up or the trail you just came down. If no blaze is apparent, read the ground. Look for footprints or some sort of trail maintenance signs such as cut deadfall or a worn path. It is very rare that you'll see nothing. If that happens, leave the group at the last blaze and look around for an indication as to where the trail is. If it's just two of you, keep each other in sight while you look for the trail, even if you have radio or phone contact. If the group is large enough, a few people can fan out and look for a sign (while others stay put), but they *must* keep the group within sight at all times. Getting lost and then losing your hikers while they helpfully wander off is completely *aggravating* and the worst situation outside of an injury that I know of. It shows a lack of control on the leader's part.

Hiking on unmarked trails is a whole different story. Many in the New York/New Jersey area are old woods roads that should be easy to follow but if in doubt follow the widest path and keep your map and compass handy. If you lose the trail, go back to the last place you are certain of and try again.

When all else fails and the bears are looking at you as if you're a giant salmon-blueberry burrito, follow water or a stream downhill since streams almost always lead to civilization in some way. Whistling in repeated clusters of three toots is a good idea when trying to be located.

As you hike, be sure to pay attention to the blazes. Don't push on without seeing one, assuming you're on the trail. Trust your instincts and if it feels wrong, there's a good chance it is.

After the Hike

Leave a change of clothing in the car, including sneakers. A fresh shirt and pair of socks will make you feel human again after a long hike. A cooler with cold water and a snack is also good to reward yourself and friends with after a summer hike. In colder weather, a thermos full of hot chocolate or tea is like a gift from above. You'll be very glad you brought it.

Using GPS

In many chapters, I've included Universal Transverse Mercator (UTM) coordinates, useful for finding sites with Global Positioning System (GPS) receivers. UTM is a digital version of the more traditional longitude/latitude system of location. The GPS code, in UTM, for the monument on Beacon Mountain is 18 T 0588074 easting, 4593497 northing. On the receiver it looks like this: 18 T 0588074, 4593497.

GPS is great at telling you where you are but figuring out where you need to go takes time and practice. In most cases, the coordinates listed throughout the book were taken by me at each site. I've marked the waypoints, such as mountain peaks, mines, trail intersections, or other landmarks I want to remember when accuracy at the time was at least 19 feet or better. GPS is not always useful for a pinpoint location but it will put you within a general area and then it's up to you. The programs I use to transfer coordinates and waypoints are Maptech Terrain Navigator and Garmin MapSource. I also get coordinates at Topozone.com. Most GPS hand-held units use WGS84 (World Geological Survey of 1984) as their default map datum, though longitude/latitude is used instead of UTM. It should be easy to convert from longitude/latitude to UTM.

To use my coordinates, follow these steps:

1 Mark a current waypoint anywhere. It doesn't matter.
2 Highlight the UTM coordinates and change them to the new coordinates.
3 Change the name of the waypoint and even the identifying symbol.

It's like learning a new language. For an excellent tutorial on GPS use, check out Garmin.com.

You can generate documentation of your hike by creating a "track." At the trailhead, enable the "track" feature of your GPS, which records an electronic "bread crumb" record of your adventure. Mark significant waypoints as you go. Stop the "track" at the finish and save it, giving it any name you wish. The unit can then tell you the total elevation changes and mileage. Transfer your new track to a mapping program, such as Maptech Terrain Navigator, and you can also transfer waypoints from the mapping program to the GPS. That comes in handy when you want to find something or have confusing territory to navigate through.

Using GPS to find sites or get out of being lost is a tremendous advantage but beware of staring down at the unit when there are hazards in the area, such as sudden drops, holes, mine shafts, or impatient hiking partners.

If your GPS has an altimeter, always calibrate it at a known value before you hike, i.e., if your front steps are identified as being at 200 feet above sea level (on a hiking map or from Topozone.com), remember to check the altitude reading and make any corrections before you go. Many GPS receivers read altitude and interpret it barometrically but as we all know, air pressures change constantly. Paper maps are always correct in elevation values. Similarly, when you change batteries in the unit you must recalibrate the compass.

The GPS is not a substitute for a paper map. I use the Garmin eTrex Vista, which allows me about twelve hours of battery time for my walk.

1
The Army Tunnels

WHERE Tackamack County Park and Blauvelt State Park, New York

WHY Long tunnels and other structures from a former rifle range

DIFFICULTY Easy, about 4 miles round-trip with minimal elevation changes

MAP None available that is accurate (except for mine)

DIRECTIONS Take the New York State Thruway (I-87) over the Tappan Zee Bridge and take the first exit on the other side, Route 9W South. Go about a half mile south and turn right (west) on Route 28, Old Mountain Road. Continue on 28 (now Clausland Mountain Road) to the parking lot for Tackamack County Park, on the right.

Known locally to dope-smoking, sex-crazed teenagers as the "Army tunnels," these odd passages through the woods are actually the remains of Camp Bluefields, a National Guard rifle range from the early twentieth century.

Camp Bluefields was built by the National Guard in 1910 as a replacement for their range at Creedmoor, NY. It also served as a WWI POW camp, according to the Army War College. No one ever seemed to be happy with the site as a shooting range. Marksmen complained about shooting at targets with the sun in their eyes and locals were upset when errant bullets overshooting the mark wound up piercing their homes. By 1912, the Guard ceased their operations. Between 1913 and 1918, the YWCA used the land as a summer camp for the children of working New York City women. In later years, it was an ROTC training camp and was then used by soldiers from nearby Camp Shanks (a major east-coast departure point for troops going to the European Theater during WWII) for training. Camp Bluefields was abandoned soon after World War II, left alone in the woods to endure the uncaring ravages of the elements and bored youth.

This particular adventure is more of an exploration than a true hike since we'll only be on one trail (the blue Long Path) going and coming. The distance isn't that great. What takes all the time is poking our noses into the nooks and crannies associated with the site. So what are we waiting for?

The only "official" map of the area that I was able to find was the New York–New Jersey Trail Conference map of the Palisades, on which the Long Path is featured as it passes through Blauvelt (pronounced "Blawvelt") State Park. The problem is that the features we're interested in aren't depicted on the map. The village of Orangetown has a parks department at 81 Hunt Road that was very helpful in my quest for maps and information on this park and also on Clausland Mountain County Park, an old Nike base nearby. The hand-drawn map they gave me had good general lay-of-the-land information but the rifle range isn't accurately represented and the location of the trails shown is also a question mark. Fortunately, we really don't need a trail map because the Long Path goes right to the middle of the site. You'll want to be sure to bring your Big Flashlight on this trip.

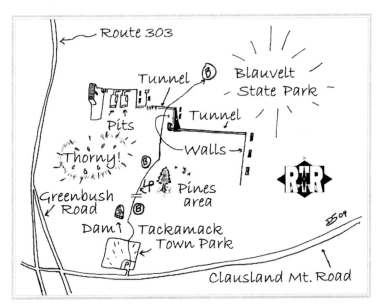

Okay then. From the parking lot, we'll pick up the blue Long Path and follow it (north) through the woods. The park, and likewise Clausland Mountain Park to the south, is named for Jan Claus, or Tackamack, the "clever Indian." He was an early landowner in Rockland County who sometimes acted as an agent in land deals with Dutch settlers. The trail passes an old dammed pond and then through a low muddy area alongside a stream. Crossing a road by some new development, the trail ascends to a stand of evergreens.

We feel that familiar "ruin sense" buzz when the trail suddenly comes upon a low wall and crosses over it. Of course, we'll leave the LP at this point and begin our investigation. This concrete "road" we're following to the right (east) is actually the roof of the first tunnel we'll find today. The entrance is at the end of the "wall" and easily located. Pulling out our flashlights, we can enter and walk the few hundred feet through to a point where it is collapsed and flooded. Beer cans and alienated teenager graffiti line the passage. As an introduction to things to come, it's exciting to explore. After turning around at the collapse, exit and then continue to the right, following along the wall. There are recesses and electrical tubing in the wall.

The targets were on two rails that were raised above the wall. After the rifleman shot at the target, it was lowered so a marker could be placed in the bullet hole, and then it was lifted back up. The rifleman could then see where his round went and take another shot.

Things get interesting quickly around here. Passing some empty blockhouses, we'll hop up onto the ledge to our right and follow it to the end. Suddenly, we're pretty high up. An opening we come across shows where a stairway used to descend to the depths of the "tower." The litter at the bottom suggests there must be an easy way down there, but how? We'll retrace our steps to where we can hop off the ledge and walk down to the base of the structure, passing a somewhat large hole in the wall along the way. No way are we climbing through there, even in the name of exploration. We do have our limits, after all . . . right?

There's another wall straight ahead, which we now recognize as the roof of another long tunnel. We'll follow alongside it and as soon as possible scramble gracefully to the top and walk along the length, passing various leftover artifacts on the ground as we go. Making our way to the end, we know the entrance to the tunnel beneath us must be here. Before we find and enter it, let's follow our last wall as it heads off to the right, passing some more blockhouses. It seems someone has attempted to make a cozy cabin of the last one.

It's now time to turn around, enter the long tunnel, and follow it back through the semidarkness to the far opening. The tunnels all have

Dave on the tunnel roof. Photo by Todd Rutt.

Army tunnel entrance

narrow window slits that allow in light and air. Surprise! We've wound up inside the base of the tower, amid the seemingly endless beer cans. What now? Explore the rooms, and yes, climb out through the hole we refused to enter just a little bit before, into the sunlight. A strange little circuit, for sure.

Retracing our steps from before, let's head back towards the first tunnel. We know we can't go through it to the end, so we'll trace it from the outside past the collapsed section, crossing back over the LP along the way. Within a short time another wall branches off to the right with two additional blockhouses standing guard. It doesn't go far and there isn't anything new in that direction, but we can go and check it out.

Right at that point, the tunnel opens again beneath the roots of a tree. Ducking down, we'll enter and follow it through the semidarkness. Deep cracks run along the middle of the walls of both sides of the tunnel, and the roof leans drunkenly. This section is obviously about to collapse at any moment and if we judge it so, we shouldn't enter. At the exit, the thorn bushes, which have been only nuisances up to now, become more problematic. Hugging the wall and doing our best to keep the blood inside our veins, let us make our way to the next corner, where more surprises await. Making the left turn, two sets of crumbling stairways tunneling under the wall appear a few yards down. Upon closer inspection, we see they lead to some sort of closed-ended pits with walls and blockhouses. We'll dutifully explore the pits and then climb back out, continuing the search forward.

At the end of the wall, at the corner, decrepit stairs lead up to a two-story structure (one level is below the one we see) whose door has been cruelly ripped from the jamb and lies buried nearby under leaves and dirt. An anticlimactic conclusion to our explorations, but that's the way it goes sometime. This is the end of the line. As explorers, we do hate to turn around and retrace our steps back to the LP for exit but those thick stands of thorn bushes will prevent us from bushwhacking back to the trail we came in on. I know this for a fact, since the RTR Investigation Team wound up bloody trying to find another exit.

I won't bore anyone with the endless stories of Satanism or ghostly haunted blockhouses that often cling to places like this. Haunted spots in the woods and empties go hand-in-hand for some odd reason. Just what *is* the connection between beer and Beelzebub? You have to work hard to attach anything evil to this place. The Army tunnels are a fascinating and unique historic site that is worthy of our attention.

2

Beacon Mountain Casino

WHERE Beacon, New York

WHY Reservoir and dam ruins, abandoned fire tower, casino and inclined-plane railway remains, little-seen Daughters of the American Revolution (DAR) monument, high Hudson River viewpoints

DIFFICULTY Challenging, about 9 miles round-trip, moderate to steep climbs and one summit scramble

MAP New York–New Jersey Trail Conference map 2, East Hudson Trails

UTM COORDINATES
DAR monument 18 T 0588074, 4593497

DIRECTIONS Taconic State Parkway North to Route 301 West, toward Cold Spring. At the intersection of 301 and 9D, turn right (north). Go about two miles past the parking area for Breakneck Ridge (once through the tunnel) and look for blue blazes on a telephone pole, just past a private home (about four miles from the intersection of Route 301). The parking area is just north of the blazed pole, on the left side of the road, about two miles south of the town of Beacon on Route 9D.

It's true that this particular outing may be shorter on things abandoned than some of the other hikes in this book, but the quality of the points of interest is high, sometimes literally. Additionally, Beacon Mountain and its twin summits are definitely less visited than the other peaks in this mountainous chain of the Hudson Highlands, thus fewer encounters with other humans could be listed in good conscience as another "why." Did I mention it's also an extremely attractive setting for a day's exploration? I just did.

Beginning on the blue-blazed Notch Trail (we also take it on the Breakneck Ridge hike), we pass by the remains of an old reservoir system on the way up. Keep all this plumbing in mind; we'll explore the system that supported it later in the day. Continue climbing on a gradual but steady uphill incline to a point where an unmarked woods road comes in to meet us, at 1.4 miles from the beginning. Again, make a mental note of the spot for later. It will all come full circle.

Stay to the right. Blazes are sometimes far apart in this section and these woods roads can lead to confusion for those hikers that are not as clear-thinking as we are. Blue always goes uphill, sometimes more steeply, and at 2.2 miles another unmarked woods road appears with trees mysteriously marked "MZR" in yellow paint. Keep this point in mind for . . . oh, never mind. This trail heads down to the Melzingah Reservoir, which we'll explore on the way back. For now, stay on blue until the yellow Wilkinson Memorial Trail joins up, named for trail builder Samuel L. Wilkinson. We part with blue and pick up yellow,

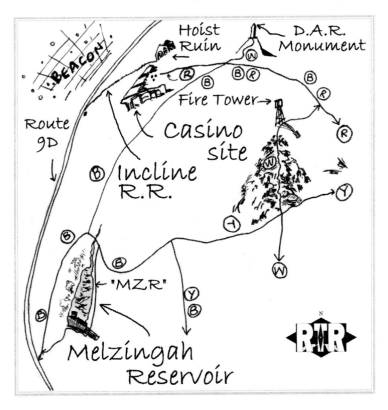

still heading north. Painted rocks point the way to the "FT," or fire tower, in this area. We're at about 826 feet in elevation.

Another intersection of trails comes in at 0.6 mile from the last one along with yet another unmarked road, which disappears into the woods on a bearing towards private property. The white-blazed Breakneck Ridge Trail makes an appearance here, on the way to its terminus on South Beacon Mountain. White and yellow travel northward together for a short time until a cairn marks the spot where white cuts to the left and goes sharply uphill and yellow continues straight. Of course, we follow the white trail as it climbs from 990 feet to 1,319, finally giving us our first viewpoints over to the Hudson River and the Melzingah Reservoir, which is between us and the river. If binoculars are available, look down at the structure on the far side of the reservoir. Some sort of building. Hmm . . . .

The Schofield Ridge, which also includes Breakneck Ridge, is to our southeast and Mount Taurus pokes its head up just behind it. The

Casino site

Fire tower

work begins again with a series of scrambles and climbs to the summit of South Mount Beacon. The fire tower comes into view on the right as we climb and once we level off, the tower is just ahead.

While we lunch by the tower at 1,639 feet, let's take in the view. Dennings Point, a new state park with camping, is the peninsula straight ahead in the Hudson. The city of Beacon is below us and the Beacon-Newburgh Bridge stretches across the river. Speaking of Newburgh, that's it directly across the Hudson from us. The casino site is at the bare patch hanging on the western end of the ledge across the valley from us, near the radio towers. To the north and west we can spy the Shawangunk, Catskill, and occasionally Adirondack Mountain chains on a clear day.

The fire tower is unsafe to climb. Common sense, even for us intrepid ruin-hunters, will take over quickly if a climb is attempted. There are signs:

Tower Closed To Public
Warning
Dangerous Structure
Please Keep Clear
N.Y.S. Department of Environmental Conservation Albany, New York 12233

Mysterious blue blazes and arrows suddenly appear along with white as we make our way (still north) down from South Beacon, heading towards the casino. We do our best to follow the white blazes on the way down but the markings come and go. If we just head downhill, we'll be fine.

At the bottom, more blue and red markings appear. This is one rare instance where these trails do not appear on the New York–New Jersey Trail Conference map but the *Walk Book* map has the red trail. Let's follow to the left (northwest) and trust our judgment as we stay on the "main" trail, now a woods road. Red heads out (in a fashion) towards the casino site and blue heads the same way but then abruptly diverts to the left (south) and drops down. Watch for the place where blue turns and descends because that's our exit later, but it also marks where we begin to look for the trail to the elusive and dimly remembered Daughters of the American Revolution monument.

When blue turns, stay on the road. Take the first right turn going uphill toward the communication towers. There are a few roads going toward the towers and it doesn't matter which one we take. At the towers, turn right and continue uphill. The first left will take us to another group of radio towers and sporadic white blazes are present in the area but can be difficult to spot if we aren't paying attention. The white blazes follow a radio tower installation fence to the summit of North Beacon Mountain, which actually is one mountain with a split summit. Following the fence will bring us to the DAR memorial obelisk (near 18T 0588074, 4593497).

The 38-foot obelisk, erected on July 4, 1900, commemorates the burning of signal fires on the top of the mountain during the Revolution. It stands on top of North Beacon Mountain, overlooking the city. From his headquarters in Newburgh, General Washington must have had a nice clear view of the fires. At one time the monument was a highlight of trips to the top, along with the casino, but these days it is dwarfed by the communication towers up there and is virtually impossible to spot from below. I get the feeling that *no one* comes up here anymore except for Daughters of the American Revolution and history enthusiasts. It isn't marked on any map of the area that I've seen. The elevation is about 1,570 feet, higher than either Breakneck Ridge or Mount Taurus.

After a short break, returning downhill to the red trail will bring us back on the road to the casino ruins. (The *Walk Book* mentions ruins of summer cottages on this road, but I haven't been able to find any.) The site of the casino will come up shortly. An incline funicular (fyoo-'nik-yoo-ler *n*: worked by a rope or cable) railway brought visitors 1,200 feet up to the casino, a lateral distance of 2,200 feet.

The casino site overlooks Beacon and affords scenic high views of the Hudson Valley. We've seen this particular panorama from the top of South Beacon Mountain.

Exploring the site, we'll find stone walls with various openings, terraced areas of concrete slab that are decaying and broken, and foundations that suggest magnificent edifices. Crumbling steps to vanished structures remain in a few different places. A broken ladder to a long-gone observation platform, rusted and neglected over the passing years, stands unusable behind the hoist house. Feel free to test your nerve but three steps are quite enough to prove this might be a good

Hoist house ruin

way to end the hike in an unhappy way. The fire tower from before is visible up on South Beacon Mountain, behind us. There is enough here to keep us happily exploring for an hour. Multitudes of different radio towers overlook the scene, intrusive newcomers to this formerly grand destination.

The Mohawk Construction Company built the incline railway in 1902 and the Otis Elevator Company contributed the machinery. Two 33-foot-long cars ran in opposite directions on a single track at a speed of 500 feet per minute with a turnout at the halfway point. A hoist assisted the cars on the way up. The casino was built at the top in 1902 and operated until a fire destroyed it in 1927. A hotel was built next to the casino in 1908 but fire also terminated that establishment in 1932. The last passengers went up the incline in 1978 but yet another fire in 1983 ended the operation forever.

The ruin of the hoist house is a prominent feature of the casino site and is unmistakable. After completing our investigation and taking pictures, it's time to start our descent but there's still a little more to see before we're done.

Take the blue trail as it drops down, down, twisting our ankles and crossing streams before finally meeting up with . . . the blue trail! Intersection of blue and blue. It isn't hard to understand why we only see the blue blazes as we're coming down. This is an unfortunate choice of color for the newly blazed descending trail and someone should change it immediately, paint the trees on both sides, and mark it on a map. The blue trail we meet is the same Notch Trail we came up on. Remember the unmarked woods road I told you to keep in mind earlier? This is it.

We could take the Notch Trail straight back to the car, but we won't. Instead, we'll bear left (northeast) on the Notch and retrace our steps to the unmarked "MZR" (for Melzingah Reservoir) woods road we passed earlier on. Yes, it's all coming together very nicely right now. Take the trail to the right (southwest) and soon the trail splits. If we go left, the trail crosses the brook and continues on the road using the path of least resistance. Of course, we'll bear right and follow the trail to a spot where it dead-ends at a brook crossing near a foot bridge that is now gone, except for the two steel rails that held planks at one time. It isn't hard to cross over somewhere else and then rejoin the old road as it heads down to the reservoir.

The final RTR exploration site for today is the Melzingah Reservoir, still serving the city of Beacon. A small but imposing concrete dam holds firm and we can now get a closer view of that square building we spotted earlier. Turning around, we look up the mountain to see if we can locate that vantage point. Were we really that high up?

There are a few dirt roads around the dam. Head over to our right (to the northern or far side of the dam) and there is a foot trail that we can pick up after hopping down to the spillway. It is plainly visible when you're there. Following the path brings us to another, smaller reservoir with broken dam structures and two pump houses, one on either side of the brook. This path leads back to the blue Notch Trail and our vehicle. The reservoir system now makes more sense to us as we retrace the blue trail downhill, past features we remember from much earlier today.

This adventure really had a nice variety of exploration opportunities. I've always liked that DAR monument in particular because I believe few people know about it or venture way up there to find it if they do. Some might ask, "Who cares?" I'd say, "People who buy books pointing out abandoned towns or iron mines might."

3

The Boston Harbor Islands

WHERE ░ Various-sized islands scattered throughout Boston Harbor

WHY ░ Extensive collection of military forts and other ruins

DIFFICULTY ░ Easy, negligible walking on each island; reached by water shuttle

MAP ░ National Park map

BOOK ░ *All about the Boston Harbor Islands* by David and Emily Kales

WEB SITE ░ www.bostonislands.com

CONTACT ░ 617-223-8666

DIRECTIONS ░ See text.

The Boston Harbor Islands offer the curious traveler a unique opportunity for discovery because a surprisingly large number of people, even from the area, know nothing of these islands. There are enough ruins and military leftovers to keep us contentedly exploring for many days, requiring frequent-as-possible repeated visits. Fortunately, we can maximize our experience by carefully taking advantage of the reservable primitive campsites on several of the islands, notably Bumpkin, Grape, Lovell's, and Peddock's. If you're exploring the islands with me, we're definitely going camping!

I'm only discussing islands that are currently served by the ferry, although virtually every island in the harbor has a ruin or structure of some sort. Access to the islands is by public or private ferries and a free water shuttle runs between the outer islands, using George's Island as a hub. In a pinch, you can hire one of the water taxis headquartered in Boston to take you out to the islands, but that's expensive. The shuttles also go to other points on the south and east ends of the harbor but there's a fee to board at those points. You can use your own boat to explore the harbor, if you have one.

The Boston Harbor Islands recently became a national park, ending the days when no one in any of the many agencies that governed the islands seemed to know how to write out a camping permit.

It's generally recommended that you don't try to see more than two islands per day, which is why camping is such a good idea; exploring your own private island after the crowds go home is quite a good way to satisfy your curiosity. Another bit of advice is to be sure to arrive at the water shuttle dock a few minutes before your boat is scheduled.

The close proximity of Logan Airport, one of the nation's busiest, should be noted since these islands can be pretty noisy during the day due to the incessant air traffic. As the big jets are coming in to land, they're low and loud and at times you can clearly see the people inside. It does get better at night but you sure do feel like you're camping on the end of the runway sometimes.

Two crucial informational resources are the main island's phone number, (617) 223-8666, and www.bostonislands.com. Research every aspect of the trip before you go. Never assume anything when making plans to visit the islands because ferry schedules or available

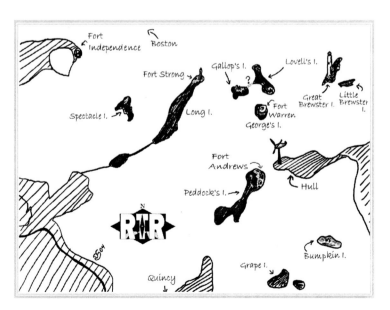

campsites can change from year to year and even day to day. Check the web site for an up-to-date ferry schedule and it is a good idea to call the main information number for confirmation.

During the summer the water shuttles from Hull or Quincy run seven days a week but after Labor Day they run on Saturday and Sunday only. After Labor Day, the boat from Boston to George's only runs on Friday, Saturday, and Sunday. Don't make a bad mistake by taking the George's boat on a Friday in late season expecting to pick up a shuttle to another island.

There are different options for formulating our plan of attack, so let's go over them:

Option 1: The most obvious choice is to take the ferry from Long Wharf in downtown Boston directly to George's Island and then pick up one of the free shuttles that go to the other islands. The big negatives for this option are dealing with nightmarish Boston traffic and the expense of garaging the car downtown (figure about $100 for two days).

Option 2: Pick up the Southern Loop water shuttle from either Quincy Shipyard or Hingham Shipyard, depending on which one is in use at the time, on the south shore of the harbor. Check www.boston-islands.com for links to the current schedule. The shuttle usually makes a run from the shipyard to Grape, Bumpkin, Peddock's, and George's Islands, stops at Hull a few times, and then reverses the route. Some of these islands are closed seasonally and the schedule is always subject to change. Parking is free in Quincy or Hingham Shipyard. You can save significant time by going directly to the campsite on one of the outer islands first instead of changing boats at George's, and there's no insane city traffic to deal with either. This is a very good option.

Option 3: Pick up an early Northern Loop shuttle from Hull at the eastern end of the harbor. The Southern Loop boat also gets there later in the day. Since both the Northern and Southern Loops service it, there are more arrivals and departures at Hull than at the shipyards. It's a longer drive to the dock but a shorter shuttle ride to some of the islands. (Peddock's is only about 0.25 mile from Hull.) That boat goes from Hull to Lovell's, Peddock's, and George's Islands and then reverses. Free parking is available near the ferry slip. This is another good option. It's also kind of neat to check out that huge wind turbine at the Coast Guard station that looks like it's about to cleave your skull in half.

Option 4: Take Amtrak from Penn Station to Boston (the high-speed Acela is expensive but a compelling thought), walk or taxi the short distance to Long Wharf, jump on the boat to George's, and then take a shuttle to your island of choice.

Before we begin, let's briefly note the five major eras of fort building in the United States:

First System: 1794–1807
Second System: 1807–1817
Third System: 1817–1876 (*Most of our ruins come from this era.*)
Endicott System: 1890–1920 (*World War I is in this time frame.*)
World War II era: late 1930s–1945

George's Island

The main tourist destination and shuttle hub (all shuttles go there), George's is the only island with drinkable water or food service. Begun in 1833, imposing Fort Warren took twenty years to complete under the supervision of West Point's Sylvanus Thayer. Arched labyrinths weave up, down, and through the fort on different levels, in similar fashion to that of the other big Third System island forts we've seen everywhere from Pea Patch Island (Fort Delaware) to the Florida Keys (Fort Jefferson). There is easily an afternoon's worth of exploring to do here and if you're in luck you might spot the Lady in Black, the resident ghost.

The fort has been restored in recent years and tours are usually offered during the summer season. As you're exploring the islands, at some point you'll wind up on George's Island.

Don't count on the island's food service or water availability for survival if you're camping. It's just not set up to supply you so bring your own.

In recent years, the Boston Harbor Association has sponsored free guided trips to George's on the second Thursday of July and August.

Peddock's Island

This is one of the largest of the islands, with a concentration of Endicott-era and World War II ruins and batteries from old Fort Andrew on the northern end. For us dyed-in-the-wool ruin hunters, this is the real deal, and we don't even have to sneak in! When exploring by the last light of day, the old gun emplacements stare balefully out at us from under their landscaped camouflage. The brick buildings high up on the north drumlin (a rounded hill of glacial drift) are slowly falling apart most artistically and are worth the exposing of some film.

The campsites are on a field close to the dock. Pitch there and visit the other islands but save the investigation of this island for after 5:00 P.M., when the ferries stop running and the crowds disappear. Do you

Peddock's Island

Peddock's building

have the nerve to explore the old batteries by flashlight after dark?

Lovell's Island

More excellent Endicott and World War II military ruin hunting is featured here. I have nothing against restoration but you just can't beat some nicely photogenic decay.

Gun batteries from Fort Standish are at the island's north and south tips, with more to discover in the middle. Centrally located Battery Burbeck-Morris is the location, in my opinion, of the entrance to the fabled tunnel between this and Gallop's Island. The most popular description of the tunnel entrance refers to a studded door at the bottom of a ladder going uphill. This would be at the first battery we come to when approaching from the south, though the door is now cemented closed.

As we walk the beach we'll discover the fallen Protected Switchboard Room used for furtive communications during the Second World War. Bring some fast film since Battery Terrill at the north tip is especially spooky in early morning light. Return to your campsite after the shuttles stop running and take the time to explore this island in detail.

A cart at the dock is available for getting gear to the campsite. The

Battery Terrill

Lovell's steps

choice sites are #6 and #7 at the end of the beach and a long walk from the dock. Site #7 is the best, being large and boasting a fine view of the harbor and the sparkly new Deer Island waste water treatment plant. Campsite #6 next door is smaller, doesn't have close beach access or the view that #7 has, but at least it's somewhat near the water. The other sites are located further inland without any water views and are tolerable camping at best. This island had the worst mosquito problem I've ever experienced.

Bumpkin

The only nonmilitary ruins accessible by ferry are here. What's left of the old hospital for paraplegic children awaits our attention at the island's high point on the middle trail; however, most of the structure has collapsed into endless heaps of brick and tile. The hospital was opened by philanthropist Albert Burrage and used from 1900 to World War I. A fire in 1945 destroyed most of the building, leaving just the shell until that, too, came down.

The trail to the lookout passes two sets of ruins, which we'll properly inspect after we set up camp. The Naval Training Station that occupied the island in 1917 covered it with almost sixty temporary wooden buildings, but the large Mess Hall's substantial foundation is all that remains of that era. The stone ruin next to it is a home from the late 1800s, which was later used as a heating plant by the children's hospital.

The four campsites on the water are the best reservable campsites on the islands: wooded, level, on the beach, and bugs were not an issue. There are additional inland sites that are also pleasant. It's another long walk to the sites from the dock but there is a cart here, also.

Little Brewster

The historic Boston Light is on Little Brewster Island. Special three-and-a-half-hour tours from Boston go out there to check out the lighthouse, which can be climbed.

Grape Island

Short hiking trails and a few unremarkable campsites are here for your enjoyment. Wild edible berries abound. This is one of the few islands with no man-made structures to see.

Castle Island

Now connected to the mainland by landfill, Castle Island's foremost claim to fame is that Edgar Allan Poe served there at Fort Independence (built under the Second System and upgraded under the Third System) in 1827 as a young man. The legend of an incident around 1817 involving a duel between two soldiers caught his attention, mainly because the unpopular victor wound up being sealed behind a wall under construction. Poe wrote his story "The Cask of Amontillado" based on the tale.

4

The C&O Canal

WHERE Washington, DC, to Cumberland, Maryland

WHY Mill ruins, aqueducts, lift lock remains, caves, huge tunnel, wilderness campsites, Civil War–related sites

DIFFICULTY Challenging 184.5 miles, 600-foot elevation change in 8-foot (average) steps

BOOKS *Towpath Guide to the C&O Canal* by Thomas F. Hahn (Harpers Ferry Historical Association), *The C&O Canal Companion* by Mike High (Johns Hopkins University Press), *184 Miles to Adventure* (Boy Scouts of America)

WEB SITES www.nps.gov/choh, www.bikewashington.org/canal

CONTACT C&O Canal National Historical Park, P.O. Box 4, Sharpsburg, MD 21782; 301-739-4200

VISITORS' CENTERS
Georgetown: 1057 Thomas Jefferson St., NW, Washington, DC 20007; 202-653-5190

Great Falls Tavern: 11710 MacArthur Blvd., Potomac, MD 20854; 301-767-3714

Brunswick: 40 W. Potomac St., Brunswick, MD 21716; 301-834-7100

Williamsport: 205 W. Potomac St., Williamsport, MD 21795; 301-582-0813

Hancock: 326 E. Main St., Hancock, MD 21750; 301-678-5463

Western Maryland Station: 13 Canal St., Room 304, Cumberland, MD 21502; 301-722-8226

Unique historic sites and prime primitive campsites make the venerable C&O a worthy destination. The Chesapeake & Ohio barge canal, in use from 1829 to 1924, runs over 184 miles along the Potomac River from Washington, DC, to Cumberland, MD. After almost a hundred years of use, floods and changing technology (especially railroads) forced it out of business. It became a National Historical Park in 1971. There is so much to see along the trail that a detailed breakdown is impractical for this book. Instead, I've outlined some highlights.

My favorite places along the canal:

1 Monocacy Aqueduct
2 Harpers Ferry, WV
3 Caves around the halfway point
4 Dam 5 and the crossover area just north of the dam
5 Lock 46
6 Fort Frederick State Park
7 Round Top Cement Mill
8 Paw Paw Tunnel

The first thing to do is to consider some logistics. Hiking the canal at an average of 10–15 miles per day means that about three weeks or so are required to do the trip, figuring in a rest day (or area exploration) or two. Biking it takes half the time. The canal towpath is level, except for 8-foot average rises at the lift locks. The path is usually composed of dirt or gravel but it can get "rooty" and rock-strewn as we move further west, and mud is always an issue. The elevation of the

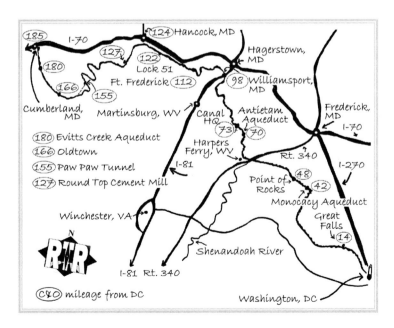

terrain is higher at Cumberland (about 620 feet) and drops as we head towards DC, so it makes perfect sense to hike or bike it in that direction. All of the tour books, however, start out in DC and tick off the miles heading west and so, for the sake of continuity, we'll do the same.

Biking is really the best way to explore the entire length of the canal in a reasonable amount of time and gives you more flexibility as to where you stay. Backpacking 26 miles to our first campsite is also a tough nut, so for my mental health we'll do it this way.

Whether we're doing the entire 184 miles or breaking it up into bite-sized chunks, getting back to the starting point is our primary challenge. Major cities along the route are Washington, DC; Harpers Ferry, West Virginia; Hagerstown, Maryland; Martinsburg, West Virginia; and Cumberland, Maryland. Amtrak (trains 29 and 30) or Greyhound serves all of them but check web sites for exact information. A private car shuttle from one of the bike shops along the route will cost about a dollar a mile, and some places will charge you for their return trip.

Making an arrangement with a shuttle service can be good, especially when you're only doing smaller pieces. Leave your car at the end point of the trail and have the shuttle bring you and your gear to the beginning of the ride. Then you bike to your car.

If public transportation is used, leave your gear at the trailhead or hotel room (or leave your partner with the stuff at one of the hiker/biker campsites), drive your car to the end point, then take the bus or train back to the beginning to start the trip.

Taking bikes and gear onto the train in Cumberland is a problem because there are no checked luggage facilities there and they won't let you do it yourself. Greyhound accepts boxed bikes but there may be a surcharge if weight restrictions are exceeded. Don't plan to go one-way by bike and expect to return by public transportation.

The Park Service information packet has campground details, camping regulations, bicycling advice and repair shops, canoeing information, boat ramp inventory, recreational facilities, and river access points to the hiker/biker overnighter campsites (for those canoeing the Potomac). They can also advise regarding towpath washouts or relocations. Floods and hurricanes have damaged the canal in the past, requiring some adjustments to the route.

Do not even consider doing the trip without a towpath guide. The different guides all have something to offer:

- *Towpath Guide to the C&O Canal* offers a complete inventory of canal structures and histories.
- *The C&O Canal Companion* gives better traveling advice than the other books.

* *184 Miles to Adventure* is a no-nonsense travelogue with good maps.

Campsites are spread out at about 6-mile intervals throughout the route, making our exploration one big exciting camping trip. Some campsites are called "hiker/biker overnighters" (H/B/O), meaning that they are reachable only via the towpath. Stays are limited to one night. A few are car-accessible, making supply drops or exits convenient. There is water (seasonal, usually turned on around April 10) at the campsites, as well as picnic tables, outhouses, and fire rings. Several sites are very close to the river, making them pleasant places to stay. Locals favor the sites closest to town. Beware of poison ivy.

The first H/B/0 is at Swain's Lock, 16 miles down, so we have our work cut out for us. Unfortunately, since it is the first campsite, it can fill early (or even be closed) so we need to be mentally prepared to go down to the next site, Horsepen Branch, at mile 26.1. Before we begin thinking about starting a little further down, understand that the first bunch of miles is interesting and worth the trouble. It's one of the few watered sections of the canal we'll encounter.

Noted miles from DC are approximate.

0 miles: Starting out from Georgetown, the towpath calmly winds through the nation's capital as it passes by apartment buildings and stores (and the Watergate) before hitting the first of the seventy-four lift locks on the trip. We also pass under several highway bridges we'd probably recognize more easily from topside. There are fourteen locks in the first 10 miles of the ride. Note how they all "rise." There is a reason saner people do the trail in the opposite direction.

14 miles: The Great Falls of the Potomac come in. George Washington's 1785 Potowmack Canal remains are on the Virginia side, an early attempt to skirt the treacherous falls of the river for cargo-bearing vessels. That canal is short and you can walk the dry canal's length from the top all the way down to the river through a deep, primitive-looking cut. At 15 miles, the Great Falls Tavern on the Maryland side is now a C&O museum and a good spot to take a break.

16.6: Swain's Lock has a concession stand and canoe/bike rentals. The canal is watered at this point. The first H/B/O is here.

22: Our first aqueduct, the Seneca Aqueduct.

26: Horsepen Branch H/B/O, more than likely our first camping spot.

35: White's Ferry. We are in Civil War country now. A concession stand and various rentals are available here. A beached ferry boat, the *Jubal Early*, is named for the Southern general who staged an unsuccessful last-ditch raid attempting to capture Washington, DC, in the final days of the war.

42: Monocacy Aqueduct, the canal company's showpiece. At 516 feet long, it is the second-largest man-made feature on the canal (after the Paw Paw Tunnel). The gracefully arched structure has been badly damaged by hurricanes and should be completely renovated very soon. Walking our bikes across, high above the water, is fascinating and a highlight of the trip.

48: Point of Rocks. There's quite a bit of activity going on here with the canal and rival railroad joining up to pass on the narrow ledge together. A (now fixed) pivot bridge, lock 28, and an H/B/O are all here. This is a favorite place for folks who live nearby to walk and bike. When I biked the canal some years ago, a youngster on a bicycle approached my friend and me and memorably asked, "Do you know any good bike trails around here?"

51.5: Catoctin Creek Aqueduct. The busy activity of the capital district is fading as the scenery becomes increasingly rural. There is a whole different feel to this leg of the trip. We are beginning the third day of the bike ride and we've seen lots of interesting locks, lock tenders' homes, and historic structures. The one constant is the Potomac.

The area around Frederick, MD, has many historic places that are worth exploring after our ride is over. Civil War enthusiasts should not miss Antietam Battlefield in Sharpsburg, site of one of the bloodiest battles of the Civil War. These days the battlefield is quiet, peaceful farmland with monuments and cannon paying tribute to the many fallen soldiers. Washington Monument State Park, east of Hagerstown, features the first monument built to honor the president. It was dedicated in 1827 and looks like a two-story stone milk bottle. The more famous Washington Monument in DC was dedicated in 1885.

57.6: Small factory ruins.

60: Sandy Hook, a good supply stop.

60.6: Bridges and remains of bridges cross the Potomac on the way to Harpers Ferry. This is the beginning of major ruin hunting and Civil War history comes fast and furious. Our old pal, the Appalachian Trail, joins in for a short time before crossing over to Harpers Ferry. There is a youth hostel near here, on the canal side of the river, which gives us some welcome relief from all the primitive camping we've done, not to mention the prospect of a real shower.

Harpers Ferry National Historical Park is attractive and a natural place to take a break from all the spine-jarring trail riding. Plan to spend a day here and take advantage of a restaurant. This is also an opportunity to learn about John Brown's famous 1849 raid on the armory along the Potomac River. Interesting mill ruins sit by the Shenandoah River and lock 33 along the canal is also a good ruin.

Write to the park for brochures and information: Harpers Ferry National Historical Park, P.O. Box 65, Harpers Ferry, WV 25425.

61: The Maryland Heights Trail (roughly 1.75 miles round-trip) runs from a trailhead accessed from the towpath and climbs up the bluff opposite Harpers Ferry, eventually ending at Overlook Cliff. Along the way, the trail passes three gun batteries and stone fort ruins.

69: Antietam Creek Aqueduct Recreation Area. Three beehive-shaped limekilns, remnants from the thriving iron-making days, are all that remain of the industrial village that once extended for a half mile along the banks of the creek. Here, iron from local deposits was forged into weapons and also the usual farm implements. The ironworks were most active in the 1840s, sometimes shipping pig iron via the canal to Harpers Ferry for further refinement. Additionally, a number of different mills at this site (grist, shingle, spinning, and saw) used water-power to manufacture their goods and the canal to ship them out. The 140-foot aqueduct is a few hundred feet south of the parking area.

69.6: Antietam Creek Ranger Station (National Park Service), 301-432-6348.

75.6: Several caves, known as the Sharpsburg Shelter Caves, are in this section.

88: More caves in this area.

This section of the canal is the first one that I explored with my friend Dave (who lived in the area) and I have many good memories of

C&O lock near Hagerstown

Towpath

days spent discovering the canal's secrets. We got muddy together crawling into caves and walking through mucked-up old locks whenever I drove down from New York City to visit him.

I found out about the C&O in a roundabout way. Dave and I are childhood buddies and when he moved down to Hagerstown, MD, in the 1980s, we wrote to each other from time to time. In one of my letters, I thought that I still had room in the envelope for my postage stamp's weight allowance and so I stuffed some Chinese food receipts, used napkins, credit card blanks, and other stuff into the envelope. In his next letter, Dave reciprocated with likewise useless junk.

One letter he sent contained a C&O pamphlet from the National Park Service plus other C&O literature. Not all the paper we packed into the envelopes was useless.

Good things were hidden between the business cards, sales brochures, and magazine tear cards. The C&O material intrigued me because I liked ruins and ghost towns even back then. On my next visit, we got the *Towpath Guide* out of a library and went to work exploring. In 1987, we biked it together end to end. Mostly.

92.11: Dellinger's Cave.

92.25: We're halfway. Three to four days from Washington by bike at an average of 25–30 miles per day.

99: Williamsport, the canal town that was the nation's capital for twenty-eight hours during the Revolution. Steel-framed Western Maryland Railroad bridges make worthy photographic subjects in the late afternoon's golden light.

106 to 109: There are plenty of lift locks and auxiliary structures relating to the dam 5 complex here to explore. Check out the ruin of the mule crossover bridge at mile 107. Four Locks at mile 109 are particularly noteworthy. We're starting to gain in elevation more seriously now.

112: Fort Frederick State Park is a restored 1756 stone fort that features summer reenactments. The park is a worthwhile place to explore while taking a break from the bumpy, muddy towpath.

116: Licking Creek Aqueduct. Ruins of the old aqueduct are near a hiker/biker/overnighter campsite. Make camp here if it is a reasonable place to break and then we can examine the aqueduct and walk down to the river. Interstate noise can at times be intrusive, however, which is the only drawback to this spot.

123: Tonoloway Creek Aqueduct and an adjoining lift lock.

123.5: Town of Hancock, MD. After following a generally northwestern heading from our start at the nation's capital, the canal and Potomac now bend more toward the west. This is a good supply point, and there are restaurants and motels in town if we need a change of pace for a night or two. The National Park Service runs a small C&O Canal visitor center and museum that we need to see at 326 Main Street, 301-678-5463.

127.4: Round Top Cement Mill. This is a major point of interest on our adventure.

Round Top Cement Mill

Inside Paw Paw Tunnel

Dating from 1837, it's the most accessible old ruin on the towpath. Interpretive signs posted along the canal tell the history of the place.

H/B/O campsites are getting more and more remote. Trains chugging through on the other side of the river are the most frequent reminder that we aren't totally removed from civilization.

154.5: A dramatic series of lift locks that are the precursor to the spectacular Paw Paw Tunnel. Once we start exploring these locks, we know the tunnel is just ahead and we've been looking forward to going through it from our first day on the path!

155: Paw Paw Tunnel. This is it, the major feature and heavy hitter of the trip. At 3,118 feet long, the tunnel cuts through the hard mountain rock to avoid a 6-mile series of bends in the Potomac.

We may want to pass through it a few times, just to take it all in. Bring a flashlight to examine the bricks lining the walls, and look for tow-rope burns on the rail. An interesting effect is the way the dot of light from the portal at the opposite end of the tunnel appears to maintain its size until we are very close to exiting. Fellow tunnel explorers' dark silhouettes against the portal openings form ghostly shapes as we walk through. Indistinct voices seem to whisper at us through the damp air near the eastern end of the tunnel.

The last 30 miles pass peacefully through the Maryland countryside towards the western terminus, where there is an excellent bike shop and Park Service visitor center.

184.5: Cumberland, MD, the "Queen City of the Alleghenies." End of the trail. Turn around and go back to DC.

5
Camp Hero

WHERE Montauk Point, Long Island, New York

WHY Remains of a WWII-era Air Force base, including radar tower building, anti-aircraft gun emplacements, various ruined buildings and structures, rumored shadow-government subterranean lab, extradimensional monster caught in a space/time warp, and secret underground submarine base. I'm not making this up.

DIFFICULTY Easy, only a few miles with minimal elevation changes

MAP Camp Hero State Park map

CONTACT New York State Office of Parks, Recreation and Historic Preservation; Long Island Region; P.O. Box 247; Babylon, NY 11702-0247

DIRECTIONS Long Island Expressway to exit 71, Route 24 South. Continue to Montauk Highway and bear left (east). Go straight for about 30 miles to Montauk Point State Park and head for the lot near the famous lighthouse. Follow the signs to Camp Hero.

For a certain segment of the population, 415-acre Camp Hero may very well be the Holy Grail of Road to Ruins exploration. Some of us got very excited when we found out it had finally been opened to the public for proper visitation (although it has been a state park for twenty years). Sneaking in is *so* 1980s.

The Camp Hero/Montauk Point area has been inhabited since the days of the Montauk tribe. The lighthouse at the point was constructed (under authority of George Washington) in 1795, and Teddy Roosevelt's Rough Riders assembled in the area for R&R sometime around

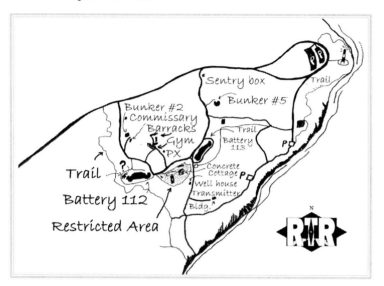

1900, following the Spanish-American War. Coastal defenses went up in 1942. The base was named for U.S. Army Major General Andrew Hero Jr., the chief of coastal artillery between the world wars.

An odd feature of the base, circa 1942, was that it was designed to appear as a small coastal village to enemy air reconnaissance. About 650 enlisted men lived amid what appeared to be peaceful Cape Cod–style homes and even a church with a steeple (actually a gymnasium). In 1947, the base was placed on inactive status and then demilitarized in 1949.

The renamed Montauk Air Force Station defended the New York area with its sophisticated new radar (the Semi-Automated Ground Environment, or SAGE, system) from 1951 to 1957. The radar tower arrived in 1960 and is 120 feet wide, 40 feet high, and weighs in at about 80,000 pounds.

From 1981, when the site was deactivated for the last time, until the present day is when things got interesting. Let me tell you the strange but true story of how I first got involved with Camp Hero.

In the spring of 1987, my friend Marcus belonged to a camera club in Brooklyn. At the same time I was studying photography at a local college and so we would go out shooting every weekend. Even back then I was attracted to ghost towns and similar abandoned locations so we would poke around places like defunct Roosevelt Raceway on Long Island, old forts, and the like. We eventually became fairly organized and did a few notably successful investigative missions in later years as the IMF Photo Team, a rotating group of urban explorers.

One night I went to a photo club meeting with Marcus. After the meeting, we went out to dinner with one of Marcus's friends from the club. I'll call him Jon. Jon was a tall, gangly guy with arthritic hands. He had been printing some shots in the club's darkroom that night and at dinner Marcus asked me, "Did you see Jon's picture?"

"No," I said, not knowing what picture he was referring to.

Jon showed me a print. I didn't think much of it, but a few days later I decided I had to see it again.

A week later, Marcus and I went over to Jon's apartment in Brooklyn to get a better look. He met us at the door and escorted us in. Eight-by-ten black and white prints were piled up from floor to ceiling in the small place. Jon pulled out a handful of prints from one stack and we went over to the kitchen table where the light was better. I got my second look.

The image was a cropped blowup from a larger frame. It showed an anti-aircraft gun emplacement (Battery 112) of WWII vintage. These batteries are sometimes referred to as "bunkers," but that terminology is technically incorrect. It looks like a big wall of concrete with an opening that's about 20 feet high from ground level, where the gun used to be. There is a semicircular brim a few feet above the opening, where a curtain used to hang, which could be drawn around the gun to hide it from enemy aircraft. The roof is covered with earth: in fact, most of the structure is camouflaged that way. So we have this emplacement, probably 40 or so feet high. Outside of the emplacement, on the left side of the picture and behind the main structure, was a figure in dark silhouette. It was about two-thirds the size of the emplacement (putting it at about 25 feet high) and vaguely apelike in appearance. It assumed a hunched-over posture, its right hand and arm appearing to be in front of the creature while the emplacement obscured the rest of the body. The top half of a rounded head protruded up from the wide, curved shoulders.

Jon had several prints (most in black and white, but some from color slides) with differently filtered exposures, contrasts, and blowups of this creature (which he called "Junior"), trying to pull some detail out of the dark shape. Junior was not giving up any secrets that way.

"What is it?" I asked him.

Jon told me that out by Montauk Point stood the remains of the old Air Force base called Camp Hero. It is state-owned property, but at the time closed to the public. He belongs to a group of researchers called the American Psychotronic Association, which uses electronics (vacuum tubes in particular are popular with them) to measure psychic phenomena. Their measurements pointed to Camp Hero and there, after gaining entry permission from the office of Senator Barry

Goldwater, they climbed up inside the radar tower building and took photographs of the area. The psychotronic investigators didn't physically see Junior behind the structure at the time, but they took panoramic photos of the area from the top and he appeared on some of their prints after they were developed.

Well, this was all very interesting, especially the description he gave of the base. I was thinking it was a place I needed to see. Of course, I had many questions about Junior, also. Jon invited us to the American Psychotronic Association's next meeting, where we could meet with them and get the answers we were looking for.

In the time between the meeting with Jon and when we actually met with the APA, Marcus and I did some homework and called the military historian at Fort Hamilton in Brooklyn. He had never even heard of Camp Hero. He did tell me that similar installations were on the Rockaway Peninsula (Fort Tilden) and at Sandy Hook in New Jersey. These places were formal parks and open to the public.

BEGIN PHASE I: PREPARATION.

Over the next few weekends we visited both places, familiarizing ourselves with the gun casemates, or "batteries." In those days (the late 1980s), Fort Tilden's batteries were closed and gated off but easy to sneak into, which we did more than once. Some go down a few stories into damp pitch darkness. Tilden also has some building shells on the surface and the remains of a Nike missile installation. It was a good place to warm up.

Some strange coincidences added icing to this unusual cake as we prepared our mission profile. I was visiting a friend of mine one day as his sisters were watching a sitcom on television concerning high school students at their science fair. As I passed through the room, one character mentioned the name of his project: "psychotronics." True, he used it to read his girlfriend's mind, but it isn't a word one hears every day. How strange that I should be passing by at that exact moment. A newspaper ran a Sunday pictorial of abandoned New York City–area military sites, including an aerial photograph of Camp Hero. Another time, when I was listening to the radio one night, searching around the dial for those low-powered stations you only hear in the early hours, I came across a discussion of the evil doings at the base. Think about it: a station I've never heard before, at a time I rarely listen, discussing Camp Hero, and I happened to stumble across the conversation. When I last went out to Camp Hero to research this book, a local newspaper was running a story on the base. Another coincidence?

PHASE 2: THE MEETING.

Finally the day came when we were due to meet with the American Psychotronic Association. The plan was we would come in after their meeting (which was closed to nonmembers due to the high security risk) and at that time ask them what we wanted to know about Junior. Marcus and I drove over to a high-rise apartment building on the west side of Manhattan. Walking to the building after we parked the car, I said to him, "This is going to be weird. We have to play it straight, and be careful not to laugh or insult them."

We took the elevator up and knocked on the door. A serious-looking heavyset fellow with jet-black slicked-down hair and dark sunglasses opened it and let us in. The group was in the living room, while three others were in a small kitchen area just beyond. The ringleader, Coynes (all names are pseudonyms), was the guy who opened the door. He planted himself on a couch and stayed put for the rest of the time we were there, sitting solo, the cushions around him pushed up in protest. His shirt was a size too small and the buttons strained to stay closed. He didn't smile once.

Another fellow, Carr, didn't seem to be unusual in any way; indeed, he seemed to be the "normal" person in that crowd. Years later, some members of this group or a similar one became involved with federal law enforcement after attempting to poison local politicians on Long Island (because they prevented access to places like Camp Hero) by slipping them radium-laced toothpaste. I believe that Carr was among that group.

There was another man there whose name I never knew. I remember thinking that if Charlie Brown was a real person he'd look like this guy. Jon was also there, blending in perfectly.

That was the crew in the living room. In the kitchenette sat a pair of older women who looked alike and never said a word, accompanied by a wizened old man, who was also quiet during the interview.

Marcus and I introduced ourselves and thanked them for their time. We told them that based on Jon's picture, our intention was to go out to Camp Hero twice: our upcoming recon objective that Saturday was to get the lay of the land, check out the base, and attempt to get a picture of Junior. Our primary mission was a few weeks later and was intended to be a more thorough penetration of the structures and an attempt to corroborate what Jon had told us.

With Coynes moderating, I starting asking questions. He seemed to be irritated and answered in short sentences, often answering questions with questions. As we began the interview, Charlie Brown pulled out a tape recorder.

"Can I tape this?" he asked.

"No!" Coynes said sharply. "Take the tape out. Show it to me." Unhappily, Charlie did as he was commanded. I was taking notes with a pen and pad, which the big man didn't seem to mind.

"What is Junior?" I asked.

We were told that he is an extradimensional being. After the military left the camp, a few years passed before another group came on the scene. Secret in nature and part of a shadow U.S. government, they were involved in mind-control experimentation using huge amounts of power. A psychic was strapped down into the "famous" Montauk Chair and huge amounts of power, generated in a building on-site, was channeled through him, sent up the antenna on the radar building, and then broadcast out over the eastern end of Long Island.

In a nearby restaurant, one moment everything was fine and calm, but then the malevolent psychic broadcast began and bedlam ensued. Fights broke out, damage was done, and people were killing each other. The experiment abruptly ended; amid the calm but bloody aftermath no one could recall what just happened. These experiments took place in the 1970s as this secret group built a research complex five stories under the ground in an attempt to remain undiscovered.

The nefarious schedule continued until the day something went terribly wrong. During a particularly powerful experiment, the unforeseen occurred. As a huge current swelled around the "Chair," a door between dimensions opened and the monstrous Junior stepped out. He went on a furious rampage, killing everyone he could get his paws on until someone managed to cut the power (with an axe to the power grid). The door closed shut on Junior and there he is to this day, stuck behind the casemate, 20 feet tall, frozen between dimensions, waiting for his chance to continue his mindless assault.

"Did you go back after getting the picture?" I asked Coynes.

"No, why should we? We got the proof that we wanted."

Marcus asked him, "Is it safe to go out there?"

"Unmarked police cars patrol the area. Whoever those cops are, they'll arrest anyone they catch trespassing on the base."

During further conversation, it was revealed that there was an underground submarine base on the site, also. They couldn't tell us where it was or how we could get into it. They told us about the radar building and the spot behind the gun batteries where Junior was stuck. They told us that radio tubes act as "psychic valves" and were useful for measuring paranormal activity.

We continued with the questions but their answers were vague and unsatisfying. As we were getting ready to leave, the old man at the kitchen table spoke up: "Would you like to consult the pendulum?" We walked over to him. He produced a sphere of wax that was about the size of a golf ball; a single strand of thick copper wire spiraled around it from top to bottom. He suspended the pendulum from his hand by a thin clear filament that looked like fishing line. Yes, we wanted to. Maybe we'd get solid answers from it. The old man started rotating the pendulum in slow circles an inch or so above the kitchen table as the group looked on and then, as he concentrated on it, he said we could start asking it questions.

"Is Junior out there at Camp Hero?"

"Yes," the old man said as he stared at his circling wax ball.

"Will we get a picture of him?" Yes.

"Will we get arrested next week when we go out there?" No.

"Will we get into the radar building?" Yes.

We couldn't think of anything else. Then the old man asked us, "Would you like me to put a dome of white light around you?" We didn't want to be rude but we had to know a little more about that!

"What does it do?" Marcus asked.

"It will protect the both of you from harm when you go out there."

We looked at each other and said, "Yes." That was it.

We left the meeting, not believing a word of this but still fascinated with the whole situation. We wondered whether Jon was going to be executed for his serious security lapse.

PHASE 3: THE RECON.

It's nearly a three-hour drive out to Montauk Point from Queens. You don't see any sign of the Air Force base until you're almost at the Point. At one particular high spot on Montauk Highway the radar building and that huge dish on the roof suddenly appear off in the distance as the drive east pushes on, but then the road dips and they vanish.

We drove slowly past the base gates along Montauk Highway once we felt sure they led into the camp. After a quick recon of the entrances, we parked by the lighthouse and got our gear together. Although the signs said clearly to keep out, the fences were bent and full of holes and gaps. Those shadow-government boys didn't keep up the housework, it seemed. Once in, we started out towards the radar building and took pictures as we went along. The place was very quiet. We heard the Atlantic Ocean crashing on the beach a few hundred yards away and the wind blowing through the trees. Sounds of cars driving on the nearby road made it seem as if those malevolent "Men in Black" police-men would suddenly appear at any moment and hustle us off to some holding cell six stories down. We walked in silence, ready to bolt into the brush at a second's notice, but we never needed to.

Radar building

It was hard to resist going into the many open buildings we passed but we had to keep our objective in mind. Infiltration of any structures would have to wait. Approaching the radar building, our excitement grew. There was an open door at the base of the building! We walked up and went inside, but not very far. We looked into the open first floor and then came out again. Stay focused. The building is on the highest point of land at the base and affords a good view of the surrounding area and the gun emplacements were in clear sight. There are actually two of them a few hundred feet apart. We both took pictures and looked over at them through binoculars but we sure didn't see any extradimensional apelike monsters hiding anywhere near them. We exited the base through another nearby gate and walked back to the car along Montauk Highway. On the way back, we checked out some old submarine lookout towers west of the base, at Shadmoor State Park. So far, our mission was a success.

A week or so later, when I got the pictures back, I almost jumped out of my skin. I did it! I had a picture of Junior! He was standing in a hunched-over opaque silhouette next to the concrete bunker, just like in Jon's picture. Marcus was with his family in Ocean City, MD, so I called him there immediately.

"Marcus! Guess who I have a picture of!"

"Me?" he said. I would have slapped him if he were next to me.

"No, not *you*, I have a picture of Junior!" We both whooped like kids. It was great. Man, were we ever raring to go back. As an aside, I showed the picture of the encasements and the shadow behind it to a

Open doors in radar building

Latin co-worker of mine. He looked at it and said "Yeti" without missing a beat.

Then it hit me. The pendulum was right. We found Junior, didn't get busted by Men in Black, and gained entry to the radar building. How long was that dome of white light good for? We were going back soon.

PHASE 4: THE MISSION.

A few weeks later, our team was completed when "G.I." Joe joined Marcus and me as we set off to explore Camp Hero properly. Joe was a tough-talking member of the same camera club Marcus belonged to and had seen Jon's picture also. Marcus had previously called Carr from the psychotronic group and invited him along. Carr's response was now that the government knew about our plans it was dangerous to continue.

"How do they know?" Marcus asked. Carr told him his phone was bugged. That was that. Carr didn't go with us.

Upon reaching the Montauk parking lot, we set out for the closest gate into the camp. Our objectives for this infiltration were:

1 Access the camp.
2 Enter the radar building.
3 Explore the other buildings.
4 Try to verify the psychotronic story as much as possible.
5 Check out the emplacements.

Junior

6   Look for the sub base.
7   Look for the secret underground lab complex.
8   Look for Junior.
9   Don't get caught.
10 Take plenty of pictures.

Entering the grounds was easy. On highest alert mode and ready for anything, the nascent IMF Photo Team walked silently in single file up the road and toward the main group of buildings. The nearby surf and wind through the trees still sounded like approaching cars. After a while we got used to it, feeling a bit more relaxed but still cautious. We entered several of the buildings, taking care not to damage anything. We all took many pictures, savoring the buildup to the first big event; entering the radar building.

The building itself is massive and gray. Standing at the base of the building and looking up, the first thing you notice is that huge ovular antenna sticking out at the top that doesn't rotate any longer but twists ever so slightly. Our side door was still open, so we readied our flashlights and helped ourselves inside. The three of us walked into the open space on the ground floor. The floor was wet. It was dark. Machinery was everywhere. As we were about to start climbing the steps to the first floor, Marcus found a breaker panel and to my amazement turned on the lights. How odd that after all these years there is still power to the building. Who pays the electric bill? Conspiracy theories are beginning to come into focus.

We started our ascent up the tower. We would enter each floor and then each go our separate ways, taking pictures and exploring in silence. Every floor had something different: dead panels of electronics, papers strewn around, and instruments long quiet all these years. Even with the lights on it was dark since there were no windows on the lower levels. Finally, after thoroughly exploring the floors on the way up, we made our way to the topmost level. It was actually the height of two stories with a catwalk halfway up, surrounding the antenna base and controls. That huge antenna was right above us. We walked around the space and did our individual explorations, and then as if on cue the three of us all came together at the same time in the center of the floor. The light of one opening illuminated the scene.

"This is too easy," Marcus said with a slightly amused look on his face.

At that exact moment, a long low groan, seemingly lasting forever, drifted through the room from one side to the other. The sound was like an old man moaning in pain, wavering only a little. It probably only lasted for a few seconds but we all looked at each other during the duration of the groan with a new concern. Suddenly, this became more than a game.

"Okay, that was weird," I said a few moments after it stopped. Silence. We were still looking at each other.

"The antenna, twisting in the wind," Joe figured aloud. Most likely he was right. It made sense.

We regrouped mentally and continued our investigation. Passing signs warning of a "Radiation Hazard," we climbed the last set of steel ladders that brought us out and onto the roof of the radar building. What a spectacular view! The Atlantic Ocean, the lighthouse, the other buildings, and of course Battery 112 (Junior's new home) were all laid out in a bright panorama below us on that sunny day. We did a binocular survey of the battery with no apparent sign of our extradimensional friend. I took a few pictures of the scene with my telephoto lens and then it was time to begin our final investigation: Junior and his encasements.

Marcus shut the lights off as we exited the building. Walking downhill, there were other buildings to check out. One had huge generators; some wrapped in paper. This was obviously the powerhouse. It was a spooky experience. Tools were left lying around. A fire extinguisher was sitting on a desk as if it was about to be put to use at any moment. A paintbrush was sitting in a can of thinner, the dust of years sitting thick upon it. This building definitely had the feeling of quick abandonment throughout, but try as we might, we didn't see any evidence of power being physically cut. (Did we interpret the APA's story too literally?) Those big generators must have been able to crank out some impressive wattage, however. If you needed big juice, this certainly was the place to get it.

After more exploration of other smaller structures, we found ourselves outside the first battery. It was most impressive up close; however, that huge open doorway in the high face of cold mottled concrete didn't look very inviting. Walking up to the entrance, we discovered that it led straight through to another opening on the other side. We went in and saw that a few feet inside and to our left was a long, dark hallway with a dot of light at the other end: the second gun position. Three flashlights quickly came out of our backpacks, flash units went on top of the cameras and we started to walk slowly down the cool, musty corridor towards Junior.

Our footsteps echoed through the square hallway as we made the journey in silence. Flashlight beams cut the darkness, sliding down walls and up ceilings, across rails and into side rooms. Corridors appeared every so often, some leading to rooms that we ventured into, others leading to rooms accessed by slits that were too narrow for any of us to easily fit through. Not even the fearless G.I. Joe dared to try. If one had to quickly exit that pitch-black space behind the slit, there would be no possible way to do it. All the rooms we checked out were completely empty and silent, as if cleared of any damning artifacts of evil experimentation.

The dot of light from the far opening widened and intensified as we neared the exit. Finishing the corridor walk, standing at the portal of the second gun emplacement, we were very aware that the focus of our quest was standing in frozen stasis right around the corner. We put fresh rolls of film into our cameras and new batteries into the flashes, as if we were loading our weapons. Again, we exchanged glances. This is what it's all about!

I ordered Marcus to go out there. He told Joe to go. Joe asked me why I didn't want to go first. We laughed and walked out together. Turning the corner, there we were, standing right in front of an extradimensional monster caught in a time/space warp. Except, we didn't see anything. We all took pictures. There was a small fire hydrant close to the ground and an evergreen in back of it. It was a darker green than the surrounding vegetation. Junior was a tree.

We walked back to the car through the base. At that point we didn't really care if Men in Black bothered us. Mission accomplished. Shedding our backpacks at the car, Marcus and I went to the snack bar at the lighthouse for a bite. I was first back to the car. Marcus came running out soon afterwards.

"Paul Simon is in there," he said. Marcus is a *major* Paul Simon fan.
"Get his autograph," I said.

"I don't have a pen." I gave him a pen.

"I don't have paper." I gave him the wrapper of the candy bar I just bought. He went back in but Paul and his lady friend had left and were heading out to the beach. Marcus didn't follow; the moment had passed.

I told this story to some co-workers in Seattle recently. When one of them, Kate, came to New York, she wanted to see Camp Hero. Fourteen years after our first mission, Marcus and I returned with Kate to the camp. (Neither of us has seen Joe since then.) "Closed" and "No Trespassing" signs were still there on the fences, as were the well-worn paths around them. The radar building entrance was sealed. Battery 112 was sealed. Holes had been pecked into the reinforced concrete as if some paranoid holdouts were still trying to find the shadow-government installation or the sub base. There was no sign of Junior, either, just like there wasn't all those years earlier.

On September 18, 2002, the New York State Office of Parks, Recreation and Historic Preservation officially opened Camp Hero to the public, although it has been a state park since 1984. Maps are available at kiosks that are scattered about the base. With the park map in hand, we can finally spend the day wandering around and inspecting the structures while marveling all the time at that huge radar building with the last intact AN/FPS-35 radar dish still in existence. The Men in Black have been evicted, it seems.

There is a parking area on Col. Daniel Wolf Road just north of the radar tower group that is a good central base of operations. Following the map we picked up at the kiosk, let's head north to the group of buildings designated as an exchange store, gymnasium, and bowling alley. All we can do is look since all of the structures are sealed tightly and none are accessible.

After poking around the area, we'll follow Col. Daniel Wolf Road (in front of us) downhill to the next right turn, Camp Hero Road. We'll walk down to a point at which the commissary building is up a hill to our right, and then head up there and look around. The map indicates that Bunker 2 is around here someplace. From what we already know about military camouflage techniques vis-à-vis "bunkers" (from all the crawling around we've done following the hikes in this book), we correctly guess that the bunker is below us and slightly to the north. When we go down there, we see it's another small sealed concrete structure. No access.

Following the fence around will bring us back onto Camp Hero Road near a sentry booth. The road goes uphill towards the tower, but we should veer off onto a red-blazed trail that circles Battery 112, passing our interdimensional friend on the far end as we circle the structure and come back to the road. Continuing uphill, when we get to the parking area for the radar tower group, we see the entire facility has been fenced off, preventing access.

Oh, the irony! In opening the park to the public, the New York State Office of Parks, Recreation and Historic Preservation made the most interesting parts of the grounds inaccessible. When the place was "closed," we had free access to all the buildings and structures and now that it's open, we can't enter any of them. And while I'm at it, is it only coincidence that the only clear views of Junior (from the top of the radar tower and the hill's high point by the entrance to the tower) are now sealed off? Is it the shadow-governmental circles within circles at work, still securing the scene of the crime after all these years? Some day, the radar building may be reopened as a museum. If so, you might see us there for the fourth time or even a fifth.

From the parking area and kiosk near the radar tower, heading south on Col. John Dunn Road will bring us by a well house and transmitter building before running into Old Montauk Highway. Bearing left (east), we'll take that trail past the fishing permit parking lot, eventually reaching Battery 216. Bearing left (northwest) on Coast Artillery Road, we'll make a quick left and then right at the first intersection we come to (Rough Riders Road) and pick up the Battery 113 trail. None of the hiking trails today, or even in the area, offer any kind of impressive viewpoints until they reach the ocean.

Back at the tower lot, we can bear right, heading straight down Camp Hero Road (which goes straight at the next intersection, past a sawhorse saying the area is closed to vehicular traffic), and investigate the old ball field and our last bunker, #5.

Turning around, we'll follow Camp Hero Road back to our car. Restrooms and picnic tables make the spot a good place for a lunch break, where we might plot future Island operations:

- Shadmoor State Park, 4 miles west off Route 27, is a small park with dramatically eroded 50-foot bluffs overlooking the Atlantic Ocean. Great photographic opportunities are here, particularly early and late in the day when the sun cuts across the dunes at sharp angles. On-site are two leftover spotting towers related to Camp Hero. They are both sealed and impenetrable.
- The Appendix, "Places That Aren't Mentioned in This Book," discusses the old Grumman F-14 works, easily visited from here if we take Route 27 to Route 24 North, into Calverton.

6

The Cornish Estate

WHERE ▪ North of Cold Spring, New York

WHY ▪ Estate and dairy farm ruins and reservoir, an insane hike up Breakneck Ridge

DIFFICULTY ▪ Moderate, 5 miles once you get up Breakneck

MAP ▪ New York–New Jersey Trail Conference map 2, East Hudson Trails

DIRECTIONS ▪ Taconic State Parkway to Route 301 West. Continue towards Cold Spring. Make a right turn (north) on Route 9D for 2.2 miles to some parking areas on the left, just past the tunnel.

While it is true you can hike straight to the Cornish estate and dairy farm ruins along the Brook Trail (red-blazed), it is far more rewarding to hike up mighty Breakneck Ridge and return past the estate on the way back. There is a sense of accomplishment in doing this that is difficult to accurately describe.

That's our plan. Keep in mind that we have to get here early since this is one of the most popular hiking trails in the area and parking fills up quickly. Don't forget to grab your flashlight. Let's tackle Breakneck!

The Breakneck Ridge Trail (white-blazed) starts on the western side of Route 9D, just north of the highway tunnel. This trail starts out steep and then goes straight up, passing by some sheer cliffs and dangerous turns so I definitely recommend doing this particular hike in good weather. Frequent scrambling, or using hands and feet to climb up, is required on this trail. The peak is only a bit over a linear mile from the beginning but the rise tops out at about 1,200 feet. Insidiously, there are four false summits with tremendous views before you reach the true summit, which really has no view.

At the highest false summit, look around. To your south, on the other side of the Hudson River, sits the United States Military Academy at West Point. On the right, we can't miss abandoned, exploded Bannerman's Castle on Pollopel Island. Straight ahead is Storm King Mountain. Mount Taurus is to the left (south) on the other side of the valley. It is higher, at about 1,400 feet, but this trail is steeper. Far below us is Route 9D.

At 1.5 miles from the start (it seems like 10) the blue-blazed Notch Trail crosses. To extend the hike at some future date, continue on past this point to a woods road 1.25 miles away. Follow that to the left, where it will connect with the Wilkinson Memorial Trail (yellow-blazed). We learned about Mr. Wilkinson in the Beacon Mountain Casino chapter. Anyway, the purpose of this extension of the hike is to lead us up over Sugarloaf North, where we will get the best possible look at Bannerman's Castle on Pollopel Island.

Francis Bannerman was a munitions dealer, who built his massive home on top of broken rock from New York City subway excavations. An explosion in the 1920s blew a wall out but it was repaired and business went on as usual. Eventually the island was acquired by the New York State Parks and Recreation Department, which removed most of the weapons and gunpowder. Not all of the dangerous stuff was re-

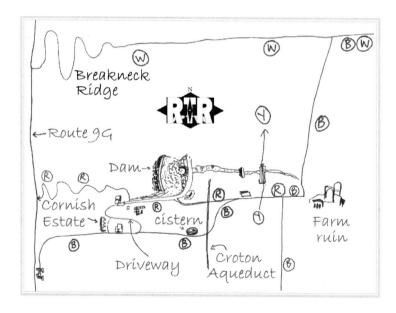

The Cornish Estate

moved, however: in 1969 vandals set a fire that touched off a massive explosion, blowing some parts of the castle across the river and onto the train tracks.

For now, let's stick to the original plan. We'll take the Notch Trail to the right (east) and follow it down to where it connects with a woods road, but stays blue.

Soon enough we see the pond, dam, and remains of the Cornish estate dairy farm. Get that flashlight ready! A massive stone barn ruin and plenty of other ruined buildings keep us contentedly exploring (and guessing usage) for a while.

The Notch turns left (east) but we will continue straight downhill on the Brook Trail (red-blazed). A concrete pump house is passed on the right. The large cylindrical concrete structure further down was a drinking water cistern, filtering water from Breakneck Brook for the estate just ahead. Explore the side trails that wander around through here, but do not get lost! We have important ruins to discover and can't waste time looking for you. The wide area we pass through on the way down is the Catskill Aqueduct.

The red trail eventually drops down to meet broken concrete pavement and the Cornish water works. To our right are the remains of another pump house, and beyond is where the brook cascades through a tunnel into the overgrown dammed pond in front of us. As

Farm site

Inside the barn

we hike down the red trail, there are two more ruined stone structures on the hill to our left that deserve our attention.

Further down the trail, the path widens and we see a structure on our right with a fallen roof. The red trail bends sharply right as it leaves the road and heads down through the woods, but we have another agenda right now. Continue straight over a concrete slab "bridge" and encounter the impressive estate, even in ruins, of Edward G. Cornish.

Fireplace

Cornish was chairman of the board of the National Lead Company, and quite wealthy. His estate dates from the early 1900s. Mr. Cornish died during the 1930s, causing the property to be tied up in litigation. It was sealed during that time but a fire in 1956 began the process of destruction that we see today. In recent years it seems that the brambles have been cleared away, easing exploration of the site. Approach the main entrance from the circular driveway. Peek over the vanished floor into the living room and check out the archways, double fireplaces, and fancy diamond tiles. It must have been quite the place in its day.

If we had continued straight past the house (instead of bearing left), we'd see a blue trail appear. Roughly 0.25 miles uphill to the left is a large, circular, rock-lined tanklike structure about 20 feet in diameter. But we didn't go straight.

Continue on the driveway, passing a once formal garden on the left, and prepare to be impressed by the huge multilevel greenhouse. With flashlight in hand, we can do a fast inspection of the basement. The driveway then bends to the right and drops through the woods to Route 9D. We will work our way around (to the left), back to the red Brook Trail, and continue down that way.

The Brook Trail brings us to the road and our car is to the right (north) about a half mile up. The best part of the walk back is passing by the incomparable Breakneck Ridge and looking up at the awesome rock face, trying to see the top, while thinking, "Did I just hike *that*?"

Cranberry Lake Preserve

WHERE ⬚ North White Plains, New York

WHY ⬚ Remains of quarry used in building of Kensico Dam, root cellar, foundations, extensive stone walls

DIFFICULTY ⬚ Easy, about 3.5 miles with minimal elevation change except for a short climb at the quarry wall

MAP ⬚ Preserve map and *History Trail* brochure, available in the nature center

CONTACT ⬚ Cranberry Lake Preserve, 1609 Orchard Street, North White Plains, NY 10604; 914-428-1005

UTM COORDINATES
Dynamite shed   18 T 0604387, 4547756
Tennis court   18 T 0604575, 4547506

DIRECTIONS ⬚ Bronx River Parkway North to the Kensico Dam plaza. Bear right at the Route 22 North exit and join up with Route 22 briefly before making the first right turn onto Old Orchard Street. The entrance to the park is on the right, and after you turn in, leave the car outside the gate at one of the pullout parking spots.

Cranberry Lake Preserve is a small (165-acre), intimate county preserve that protects wetlands near the Kensico Reservoir. Farm site and powder storage shed foundations await our attention within, and there is also an old quarry with some interesting artifacts to seek out.

The nature center hours are currently 9 A.M. to 4 P.M., Tuesday through Sunday (seasonal hours) but one can park outside the closed gate and hike in anytime from dawn to dusk. If we time our visit correctly, we can see the center first and then explore the preserve.

We'll begin by hiking on the red "Long Way" trail (just before the gate on the left) and make our way in a southerly direction towards the nature center. All of the side trails we encounter at the beginning of our trek (which branch off to the right from the red trail) will head towards the center, so we don't have to be concerned about finding it. Another point of information that we should be aware of is that the green blazes do not really mark a trail: they radiate out from the nature center to any point in the park. (The green blazes are not on both sides of trees as other colored blazes are.) Thus, to return (or if someone else gets lost or disoriented), just follow the green blazes back to civilization.

Arriving at the nature center, we can stock up on maps and other reading material and then start our adventure. They have a free black

Cranberry Lake Quarry

and white park map available inside but be a sport and buy the excellent large, color orienteering map for a few dollars. It's much clearer and will help you navigate around the trickier sites. It's worth mentioning that food is not allowed on the trails.

Beginning our stroll down the major gravel road that passes the nature center (yellow-blazed), we will then bear easterly (left) on any trail we like as we head towards the lake. Once there, we'll find the blue Littoral Trail ('lit-tər-əl adj: of, on, or along the shore). Turn left (north) and follow the trail in a clockwise direction as it circles the lake.

It can get muddy as the trail skirts the lake, sometimes on board-walks. In summer the bugs make their presence known as they greedily seek out a free hot lunch. Spring and fall are more tolerable. Blue continues to hug the shoreline until the red Long Way trail (heading southwesterly) again reappears. Let's hop over to red and begin a gradual climb, watching the high ridge on our left as the trail and the ridge eventually level out together. As the climb gets underway, through the woods we can spot a rectangular concrete support high on a hill to our left. At a point where the red trail summits at an overlook, a wide path will appear on the left. Let's note our location as we head off into the quarry area.

The quarry supplied granite to the builders of the nearby Kensico Dam. Construction began in 1913 and ended three years ahead of schedule in 1917. After being dynamited free, the stone blocks were carried by a short rail line to an immense crusher capable of processing as much as 250 tons of stone per hour. The processed stone was carried to the construction site a mile away by railroad, now long gone but easily traced. (Guess what we're doing later?) The crusher and most buildings were removed by the contractor after the dam was completed per their agreement with the county. Some structures survived, such as stone cutting and dynamite storage sheds, until they were removed in later years.

By now you've doubtless noticed the purple History Trail blazes in their artful logo on the trees. We'll follow a little chunk of that new trail but not the whole trail because the blazes are easy to lose a little further on. Bearing eastward into the quarry, we'll temporarily bypass the blazed trail and head straight towards the cliff face. A visible path goes straight to the chopped-up granite hill that supplied the stone. Very *Planet of the Apes*–looking. After snooping around on unnamed paths that snake around the base of the wall, let's turn around and go back to purple.

Turning to the right (northerly), we'll follow the purple History Trail blazes on a straight path past some stone blocks in a swampy area. We can soon see to our left the top of the support we spotted earlier and five shorter supports alongside it. This was the site of the stone cutting shed and the rail that brought blocks there from the crusher. Lots of cut stone blocks lie about, some appearing to be foundations or supports.

The purple blazes continue around the quarry and lead us to the top but soon peter out, leaving us on our own. By shading to the right, we'll get the first high views of the hike today, at 465 feet. Various bent steel rods and beams are imbedded in the stone, formerly anchoring the heavy equipment that quarried and moved the liberated stone slabs. As we pick our way along the top, the blazes will kindly reappear and lead us down the left-hand side of the quarry wall into the center of the former operation. Before we descend, though, see that checkerboard-painted rock on the western side of the quarry, down there by the pond? We're going to head over there right now.

Once we climb back down, circling to the right around the cliff face on a sandy path next to another quarry pond brings that funky checkerboard rock into view. If we pick our way along the pond's shoreline, we'll find our way over there. Steel wedges are still embedded in the granite just behind it, never having completed the splitting of the rock.

There is one more mystery we need to investigate before we're done with the quarry. Retracing our steps, we'll circle the quarry pond clockwise, passing a sandy area as we go. Bearing westerly on the path of least resistance brings us to a bona fide oddity, a tennis court (18 T 0604575, 4547506) in the middle of nowhere! As we walk around, photographing the decaying vine-wrapped fences and interior, I'll mention that the North Quarry Swim Club operated here until 1997, using the old ponds for recreational purposes. There was a diving board at the deep end of the pond. Some changing buildings were removed when the club closed, but their tennis court remained.

Although the purple blazes head off to the left (southwesterly), then turn right at a ravine and wind up downhill at the cataract, they are occasionally easy to lose and if you aren't familiar with the preserve things can get dicey. Therefore, let's continue straight past the tennis court (still heading west, with a slant to the right) and look for the old railroad bed, paralleling a low rock face. Following it to the right (northeast) will bring us back to the purple History Trail, which we can take (to the left, or westerly) back to the red Long Way path.

Once we make our way back to the Long Way, let's continue southwesterly (to the left) and arrive in time to a bench sitting along-side an attractive cataract that flows even in drought conditions. Nice spot for a break.

Continuing on red, we're now following the grade of the rail that brought processed granite from the crusher (now above us to the left) down to the dam. The rail terminus was around here somewhere, at the northwest end of the crusher. Shortly, we leave red and pick up another end of the blue Littoral Trail, which bears westward past a wooden observation tower that just begs us to climb up for a quiet view of South Pond.

Staying on the blue Littoral Trail, the low boardwalk carries us just over the South Pond's surface when we resume our walk to the west. South Pond is artificial, created in 1913 as the newly built railroad grades pooled up Cranberry Brook. If we walk quietly over the board-walk in summer, we will spot all kinds of small wildlife in or near the water: fish, frogs, chipmunks, snakes. Some exit the locality with a splash as they do their best to avoid us.

We soon arrive on the other shore. Surely there must be some sort of ruins on this side of the pond to entertain us? Possibly. When the blue trail hits the other end of the railroad grade, stop for a moment. Looking westward, we can see where the rail right of way continued straight, passing through a cut on its way to the dam.

Let us bear east (to the right) at this junction, back onto the wide gravel railroad grade. Take it a few yards down to an orange trail inter-section.

A left turn (north) will quickly bring us past the interesting 1853 root cellar and home foundation of farmer Thomas Cunningham. We can go in the root cellar and play.

Much of the preserve is on land settled as early as the 1800s. Over the years, old farms centered on the lake were combined to form large

Cunningham farm's root cellar

estates. William R. Smith bought up some sizeable property in Cran-
berry Lake with the intent of reselling it in smaller parcels but the Great
Depression ruined those plans and forced him into foreclosure. The
Strauss family eventually acquired the land and sold most of it to
Westchester County in 1967.

Why don't we take the orange trail (north) and follow it over the
boardwalk and through some swamp and then over the Bent Bridge.
Back again on the wide gravel yellow-blazed path, we now have to find
the dynamite storage shed site. For a small park there sure is a lot to
see around here. With our backs to the Bent Bridge, face west and cross
over the low stone wall in front of us. Walk about 50 feet in, with a
little "English" to the left, and we'll come across a cleared, slightly
raised rectangular area outlined with sand. This is the site of the dynamite storage shed (18 T 0604387, 4547756). I've been told a spur from
the dam railroad extended to the shed but little evidence of that
remains. The building had low 2-foot-thick walls filled with the sand
that still remains after the building was disassembled. The walls supported a wood roof, which would blow off if the dynamite exploded
prematurely, the blast being contained and directed upward by the
walls. This was our last scheduled site for today, but I'm not done yet.

Because it's a nice day and we still have some energy left, I think
what we'll do now is make a right turn (south) on the yellow trail and

Tennis court

follow it back to the railroad grade intersection. We'll follow the grade
in the direction of the crusher (left, or southeast), this time passing the
massive foundation as the path turns to hiking trail (red-blazed) on its
way to Hidden Pond. The woods around here are somewhat muddy,
usually very quiet (air traffic from Westchester Airport nearby does
intrude from time to time), and extremely pleasant to hike through,
with nominal elevation change. Once around Hidden Pond (which is
outside the preserve on White Plains watershed land), bear left on red.
Green blazes appear at that intersection, where the trail also splits to
the right towards home.

This route will bring us to old stone walls that go on and on,
marking property lines from another time. These impressive walls are
being battered mercilessly by falling trees. Having no mortar or cement
to hold them together, the walls lose. The red trail eventually becomes
the Sunset Alley Trail (still red), which runs alongside the walls for its
entire length, too soon bringing us back to our car.

8
Dennytown Mines

WHERE ▪ Fahnestock State Park, New York

WHY ▪ Four iron mines, homesite ruin, lonely millstone, site of Dennytown

DIFFICULTY ▪ Moderate, 8 miles with frequent ascents and descents. No major elevation changes but many hills and some bushwhacking.

MAP ▪ New York–New Jersey Trail Conference map 3, East Hudson Trails

UTM COORDINATES
Dennytown Mine   18 T 0594994, 4586311
Mine off AT   18 T 0596462, 4588155
Railroad bed at AT 18 T 0596635, 4588129

DIRECTIONS ▪ Taconic State Parkway North to Route 301 West, towards Cold Spring. Find Dennytown Road at about 3.5 miles down, and turn left (south). The second parking area, 1.1 miles in, is our start point. The stone utility shack off the road distinguishes the parking area. Look for the lonely ruin of an old stone lodging house just behind the shack, set back a bit into the field.

The miles go by fairly painlessly on this marathon exploration, and the points of interest are nicely spaced apart to keep things interesting. This park has the most impressive grouping of iron mines and related sites on the east side of the Hudson that I can think of. Explore this park and save the buck toll on the Bear Mountain Bridge!

Dennytown itself is long gone. French settlers in the 1880s farmed the area and cut mines into the hillsides, extracting magnetite ore that

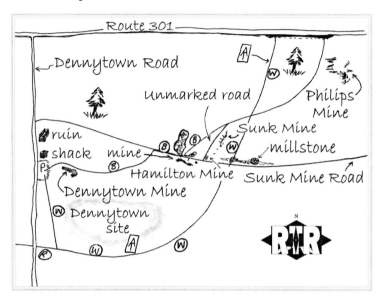

wound up at, among other places, the West Point Foundry. As we start off heading northward on the blue-blazed 3 Lakes Trail, we'll spot the clearing ahead that looks like a swamp. That is the Dennytown site. Maybe there are foundations in there, but I'm not willing to slog through mud and evade ticks to find out.

So, Dave, someone might ask, "Why are we here?" Mines! We love mines, and this park has some that we just can't pass up. Barely a half mile into the hike, we hit our first hill and begin to climb. After a short but steep climb through a narrow crevasse up to about 1,020 feet (we started at 820 feet), the blue trail tops out and bears sharply left near a tree with stones piled at its base. At this point look for the tailings pile (waste rock removed from the mine) and head in a general northerly direction to get to the beginning of the Dennytown Mine trench (18 T 0594994, 4586311). Follow the trench for about 40 feet and it ends in an impressive circular pit about 10 feet deep.

Continuing on the blue trail, we will soon cross Sunk Mine Road. Follow the blue blazes as it parallels the road and borders John Allen Pond. The trail crosses a stream near an attractive dam that acts as a spillway in high water. We can go to the edge of the pond for a fine (if early) lunch break. Either way, after a short pause along the water, go back to Sunk Mine Road and continue in the same direction as before (east).

Walking along the road we'll come to another, smaller pond. Just as the pond comes into view, we should look for a car pullout on the

Dave crossing
a bridge.
Photo by
Marcus
Lieberman.

Marcus

left side of the road that goes to the water's edge. If we stand at that point, looking to the right we can see a faint trail heading off into the woods. Let's follow it to where a wall of rock splits the short trail into a T. To the left and right runs a mine cut that isn't on the Trail Conference map. When our investigation of the cut is finished, we'll go back to the road and continue on our way.

At the end of the next bend, be on the lookout on our right for a notable homestead ruin. Stone walls mark the location from the road and a somewhat brambly path is visible that leads us into the site. A well is up the short path on the left. A clearing soon opens to reveal walls that rise up surrounding a sunken area that shows where the house itself stood. Red tiles forming a patio of sorts are at the eastern end of the depression. Let's get back to the road; our next mine is just ahead.

Down Sunk Mine Road a short distance, over a bridge crossing a stream is an unmarked trail on our left (north) side. The Hamilton

Mine cut is a few steps up the road and off the trail, so look for the rock tailings that give the location away. This is surely one of the easiest mines to locate that I know of. The mine is a narrow cut along a hillside and looks deep but flooded. All these mines are iron or magnetic iron: we are, after all, in a part of the iron-rich Ramapo Mountains/ Hudson Highlands (they're close cousins).

We'll take the unmarked road northward. As we're walking on this trail, we'll come across infrequent white square blazes. Continuing north, at about 0.4 miles, our next target comes in, heralded by an unusual sign:

Dangerous Conditions
Absolutely No Access to This Area Permitted
New York State Office of Parks, Recreation and Historic Preservation
Taconic Region, Staatsburg, NY 12580

Well then, we'd better stay out. If we continued past the sign on the faint trail worn into the rock, just over the ridge we'd probably see the huge Sunk Mine cut on the hillside far below. One imagines it would be a long, painful fall down onto those hard, sharp rocks if we were foolish enough to get too close to the edge.

I should state, at this point, that the Trail Conference map is absolutely correct in regard to where it pinpoints all the mines we're looking for today.

The unmarked road continues northeasterly past the Sunk Mine and then becomes indistinct. We'll bear left at a rock face just past the mine. Look for cut deadfall to locate the path, which bends in a northwesterly direction and narrows to a footpath, sometimes with those white squares pointing the way. Without warning, the blue-blazed 3 Lakes Trail junction appears and we're back on track.

From this point, our trail follows the blue blazes through the laurel for 2.5 miles. Continue past the Appalachian Trail junction. At a point 0.5 miles before meeting up with Route 301 we'll pass the remains of the Philips Mine, a series of mossy tailings piles, trenches, and cuts that parallel the path. It's interesting to investigate the site but we keep looking for some big feature that just isn't here. Just before encountering Route 301 bear left (southwest) on a dirt path for 0.2 miles and pick up the Appalachian Trail as it heads to the left (SSE) into the woods. Once we pass the trail register, things pick up again.

The AT follows the former right-of-way of a narrow-gauge, mule-powered railroad. The beasts pulled ore-laden cars from the Sunk and Canada Mines up to a point near Route 301 on this track. (The Canada

Millstone

mine is near Pelton Pond.) Following the railroad bed can be entertaining as we look for rock-blasting drill marks in the craggy face to our right (west). Some remarkable grades and fills keep our attention as we go along.

We'll stay on the AT as it drops through swampy hemlock stands and ascends towards fine mountaintop viewpoints across the valley to Candlewood Hill (eastward). Before that, though, there is an impressive unmarked mine cut that we need to check out while we're here.

As the trail drops through the hemlock, be aware of a point at which the stream on our left expands into a swampy area. The apparent remains of a railroad bed are on the right (18 T 0596635, 4588129), just past thick briars we passed through on the AT. We will turn right (SE) and follow the bed to the short tailings pile of black rock we see just ahead. Tailings, also called overburden, are waste rock that has been removed from the mine opening and dumped nearby. Learning to recognize tailings is a major way to locate hidden iron mines, as well as find the old roads that will frequently lead us to them. Up on the hillside is more spilled overburden, which we'll climb. Some of the rock up here is alarmingly loose as we scramble to the top. Once up, the impressive 150-foot-long (or so) mine cut (18 T 0596462, 4588155) reveals a sharp 40-foot drop down to the flooded shaft below. There are a few other holes and cuts to examine uphill from here but extreme caution must be taken when scrambling around to prevent potentially fatal slips on the loose rock and dirt. The wide mine opening is right below us.

After a careful descent, we're back on the AT. This part of the park has a remote and primitive feel to it that is very pleasant to experience. Shortly before the trail meets Sunk Mine Road, a wooden footbridge crosses a lively cascade. A sign to our left states:

Area Closed
Wildlife Habitat Recovery Area
Do Not Enter
Thank You

If we followed the cascade downstream some yards to a point where the falls slacken off, we'd find a complete but broken millstone sitting in the still water among the rocks. The last 1.5 miles of the AT will get us 1,061 feet up before the trail dips and we return to our starting point. Beware of the red Catfish Loop Trail, because the AT makes a sharp right-hand turn towards the parking area at that point. We'll pass through some old Dennytown stone walls as we finish up, and we'll get another close view of the town clearing.

Nice day in the woods. We deserve some dinner in historic Cold Spring. Come to think of it, the West Point Foundry hike is over there.

9
Doodletown

WHERE ▪ Harriman State Park, New York

WHY ▪ Town site, foundations, abandoned stairways, two mines, two cemeteries, old roads

DIFFICULTY ▪ Moderate, about 6 miles round-trip with some hills and a climb to the Doodletown Mine

MAP ▪ New York–New Jersey Trail Conference map 4, Harriman/Bear Mountain Trails

UTM COORDINATES
Doodletown Mine   18 T 0583356, 4571655
Mine Road at trail   18 T 0583589, 4571893
Edison Mine   18 T 0584458, 4571761

DIRECTIONS ▪ Palisades Parkway North to the traffic circle near the Bear Mountain Bridge. At the traffic circle, take Route 9W South. The hiker's parking area is about 1.4 miles south of the Bear Mountain Bridge traffic circle on Route 9W, just before the road into Iona Island.

There are few standing ruins left at Doodletown. What makes this hike interesting is the human history associated with the area, along with some scattered remains of yesteryear: stairs to nowhere, foundations of long-gone residences, an elusive iron mine hidden on the north flank of West Mountain, Thomas Edison's experimental mine, and the two historic cemeteries that are still in use. Photographic opportunities abound. Doodletown is a genuine ghost town, vintage 1965.

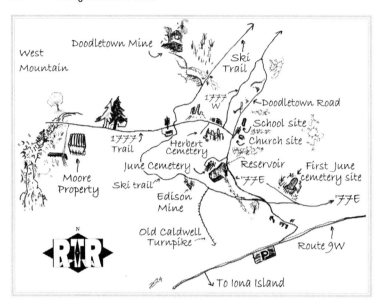

The great thing about hiking in Doodletown is that there is always something more to see next time. I've been exploring the area for years and continue to come up with new discoveries. Foundations and wells still lurk amid the sharp barberry bushes.

At the hikers' parking area, we'll cross 9W and pick up the blue-blazed trail near the sign for the merry-go-round (at the Bear Mountain Inn) to the right of the brook. The path makes a steep hundred-foot climb on decayed blacktop before leveling off near the foundation of the Gray home. This area was known, appropriately enough, as "Gray's Hill." A number of foundations and stairways are on both sides of the trail as we make our way to the reservoir, dam, and second school-house sites.

Ancestors of the June family, Huguenot in origin, first settled in the area in the mid-1700s. According to the *Walk Book*, the name of the town may stem from the Dutch first encountering the area after a fire and naming it "Dood dell," or "dead valley." English settlers added the "town" suffix in later years. Some well-known Doodletown residents included the Jones, Stalter, Herbert, Youmans, and June families; area landmarks such as Jones Point carry on their legacy. The men of Doodletown worked through the years at the nearby iron mine, on road-building projects in the area, and as grape pickers on Iona Island in the Hudson River.

Doodletown was the last parcel of land to be acquired by the Palisades Interstate Park Commission as it formed Harriman State Park and Bear Mountain State Park. The commission generously offered the fam-

ilies the option of accepting fair market value for their homes if they
agreed to sell or face the threat of seizure by eminent domain if they
refused. One by one, bit by bit, everyone sold. The final parcel of land
was acquired in 1965, finally ending over two hundred years of the
little town's existence. Many descendants of the dispossessed Doodle-
towners still live in nearby towns, such as Fort Montgomery.

We eventually meet up with the 1777E Trail, one of the four
bicentennial commemorative trails in the park (1777 East and West,
1779, and Anthony Wayne). We'll do the history lesson a little later
when we get deeper into the town site. Wide Lemmon Road comes in
and heads to the right, passing the former tree nursery, concrete-
capped reservoir, and the ski trail that skirts the first June cemetery
sites, but we aren't doing that today.

The interpretive signs that are posted around are relatively new and
take the guesswork out of our explorations. My only complaint, admit-
tedly minor, is that these helpful signs intrude on our photography. I
wish they had been placed a little farther from the features they explain.

We soon come to a T intersection, with a sign pointing out:

← June Cemetery
Historic Sites →

We'll bear to the left and respectfully inspect the second, relocated
June cemetery. The first was on a rise above Gray's Hill, and signs near

Doodletown

the Lemmon Road intersection will bring the adventurous hiker there if
there's interest, although nothing but a marker remains at the site. Flags
and flowers remind us that this is still an active burial ground and the
diminutive cherubs marking some graves are poignant. On one recent
visit, a large black rat snake was soaking up some sun in a bush beside
the road. Copperheads and rattlers are also known to be in the area.

It's time to retrace our steps and head 0.3 miles in the direction
that the sign pointed toward the "historic sites." At the wide intersection of Doodletown Road and Pleasant Valley Road (beautiful downtown Doodletown), we'll take a short break and check out the map
posted there. The red posted numbers we encounter as we nose
around are ski trail identifiers. Elevation here is about 280 feet.

More interpretive signs mark long-gone properties. How sad that
the little village was made to disappear. I'm sure that by now, if Doodletown were still around, some enterprising villager would be selling ice
cream and hamburgers in the summer and hot chocolate in the winter
to hungry hikers.

Following the 1777E Trail south, it soon splits when the '77 West
heads west as it circles Bear Mountain. For now, we'll pick up the '77W
and follow it through the woods and over a brook on a wooden bridge
as it gently climbs up to a point where it meets Doodletown Road and
the yellow-blazed Suffern–Bear Mountain Trail. We did this so we can
now follow Doodletown Road to the east and downhill, passing a part
of the old town that once had many residences. Some remnants, however, await our attention.

The Bambino homesite is marked by an interpretive sign and iron
rails imbedded in the path. We'll encounter additional foundations and
more steps to missing homes as we approach the signed "District #7"
school site, where there once stood a large stone structure that was the
pride of the town. The church site is just a few steps down. After
Doodletown was abandoned in the mid-1960s, the park used the various standing buildings, schools, and churches as garages and residences
for workers. Decay and vandalism forced razing of the structures, such
as the school, in the late 1980s.

Arriving back at Pleasant Valley Road, we'll again bear south, this
time passing the '77W intersection but soon coming to the signed
entrance to the Herbert Cemetery, the older of the two graveyards we'll
explore today. It is still active, and some area people have permits that
allow them to drive in. Look around; there is a fascinating mix of historic and modern gravestones here.

Continuing south on the '77, paths and steps are everywhere.
Long gone are any homes or structures but the Thomas property (identified by a sign) has a ruin on the hill just above the path.

Herbert Cemetery

At 0.3 miles past the Herbert Cemetery, a ski trail, marked by another map/number board, crosses our route. This is a good spot to take a break and talk history for a bit as we look for redcoat footprints in the soil.

On October 6, 1777, two thousand British troops under Sir Henry Clinton marched north from Stony Point, briefly occupying Doodletown. After a short skirmish with a small group of Continental soldiers, they headed north and then divided into two columns, taking the now commemorative 1777 East and West Trails. One column circled Bear Mountain to the west and attacked Fort Montgomery (north of the present Bear Mountain Bridge). The eastern column attacked Fort Clinton (where the bridge is today), gaining control of that section of the Hudson River.

Face south. Look up to your left (southeasterly) through the trees and identify the cleft summit of Dunderburg Mountain. Though designated on the trail map both as Bald and Dunderburg Mountains, it's actually just Dunderburg with two peaks. To our right across the valley is West Mountain, which sports a historic shelter on the south end and an impressive iron mine on the north side, which we'll visit a little later. Pleasant Valley lies straight ahead of us between the two peaks.

Continuing south on the 1777 Trail will soon bring us to a pair of spruce trees flanking a paved path (on the right). Walk down this road for a few steps and see the small, deep cellar hole of John Stalter Jr.'s home. There are other house sites down this path but little to actually discover. Nature has reclaimed this part of Doodletown.

Let's go back on the path and turn right (south). The pavement ends and the path is sometimes flooded by Timp Brook. At 0.6 miles from the intersection of the ski trail, we arrive at the remnants of the Moore property on the left. Originally a residence that was later a children's summer camp run by Riverside Church in New York City, the camp operated from 1932 to 1953. Previous versions of the New York–New Jersey Trail Conference map for Harriman State Park list the still-standing garage as a shelter. The latest reprint does not.

This is also a fine lunch spot. When the cascade is running it is quite pleasant to linger along the bank and think of the once vital village that used to exist here. This is a popular destination, however, and on weekends we will most likely have to share our quiet place with other hikers or overnight campers.

Some great features still await our presence, so let's get going. Backtracking northward on the '77, when we get to the ski trail intersection let's pause for a moment and check out the Scandell home foundation, once again marked by a sign. Heading up the short hill on an obvious path brings us to an impressive house foundation and water pump base.

Back at the ski trail intersection, it's time to hit the mine. This is a highlight of the trip as far as I'm concerned. Following the ski trail 0.3 miles west from the Pleasant Valley Road intersection will bring us to the mine road on our left (the south side of the trail), which is a few yards before a small wooden footbridge over a stream (use 18 T 0583589, 4571893 to find it). Looking carefully, we'll see the mine road joining the ski trail at about a 45-degree angle to the right (in other words, it is not at a right angle to the trail). The old mine road

Todd at Doodletown mine

can be a challenge to follow as it sweeps to the left around a knoll, crosses the brook and follows cairns in a generally southwestward direction towards the mine.

This mine can be tricky to locate so please don't feel bad if you have trouble finding it. Usually we begin by looking out for the mine road or some tailings (also known as overburden, which is rock removed from the mine and usually dumped downhill), but the trail up can sometimes be indistinct. Trust the Trail Conference map; it places the mine perfectly. Luckily, this time out we have a good leader who follows the cairns marking the mine road up to a point where the black tailings pile suddenly presents itself to us intrepid mine-hunters. Success! Climbing to the left of the tailings dump and then turning to the right once on top, we finally get to check out the mysterious Doodletown Mine (18 T 0583356, 4571655) just past a fire pit.

Special note to hike leaders: Be prepared and bring a strong magnet with you for this part of the trip. Check the dark gray rocks in the mine dump vicinity for magnetic attraction. Get your compass out and wave some ore around it to see how the different poles on each side of the tailing affects the needle rotation. I dropped my magnet into the tailings pile and it came out absolutely covered with iron material, attracting large ore-laden chunks with a satisfying clank.

The mine is a long trench cut into the hillside, flooded at the far end, where it widens out and descends into the vein. It was most likely an iron mine active in the 1800s, and quite probably even before that, during the early days of the town. Sitting about 630 feet up and surrounded by forest and running water, it's a natural spot to take a break. After careful exploration, let's return to the ski trail, passing Pleasant Valley Road as we make our way to our next mine. Doodletown Mine is quite excellent and you *will* want to return here. Guaranteed.

Walking 0.7 miles through forest down the wide ski trail, we approach the Edison Mine (18 T 0584458, 4571761), which awaits us up a hill on the right side (east) of the trail, just a few tenths of a mile southeast of the June cemetery and reservoir dam. It's a large circular cut, betrayed, as usual, by the black rock dump spilling down below it.

Thomas A. Edison had an experimental magnetic ore separation technique, and this was an early attempt to find an iron vein on land he owned in order to test the process. In later years he used his separator at the Sunk Mine in Fahnestock State Park, the Sterling (Forest) mines, and also at a larger plant near Ogdensburg, New Jersey, that processed the iron into round "cakes" (instead of the more traditional "pigs") using yet another process he developed. The cut didn't yield much iron; our compass and magnet verify that.

After our mine inspection, continuing along brings us by the old Caldwell Turnpike intersection and then a concrete bridge that spans a lively waterfall. The pooling waters down below the falls were known to those long-ago Doodletown children as the "Ten Foot," a favorite local swimming hole. In short order we come back to the broken asphalt of the 1777 East Trail.

The '77E goes straight uphill towards Fort Clinton, but unlike the British we're turning right and retracing the old road back to our car and the modern world.

10

Dunderburg Spiral Railway

WHERE ▪ On the east face of Dunderburg Mountain in Harriman State Park, New York

WHY ▪ Abandoned railroad tunnels, grades, and rights-of-way; deep iron mine shafts

DIFFICULTY ▪ Challenging, about 8 miles round-trip with some steep hiking

MAP ▪ New York–New Jersey Trail Conference map 4, Harriman/Bear Mountain Trails

UTM COORDINATES
Cornell Mine (lower)   18 T 0584489, 4570871
Trail to Cornell Mine   18 T 0584553, 4570851

DIRECTIONS ▪ Palisades Parkway North to the traffic circle near the Bear Mountain Bridge. Go south on 9W for about 3 miles to the large parking lot on the right where Routes 9W and Old 9W meet. There is a brown sign at the southern end of the lot that reads, "Vietnam Veterans Memorial Highway."

We have plenty to see on this trip, with the star attractions being the features associated with the Dunderburg Spiral Railway. Back in the 1870s, Henry J. Mumford successfully operated a tourist switchback railroad in Mauch Chunk, PA, and decided to try it here for the delight of hard-working New Yorkers. It was intended to have been drawn up by cable to the top of Dunderburg Mountain and gravity-fed in a spiral, meandering path back down to a tunnel at Route 9W. Construction began in 1890 but the project was abruptly stopped in 1891 due to a recession. After an investment of about a year's work and a million

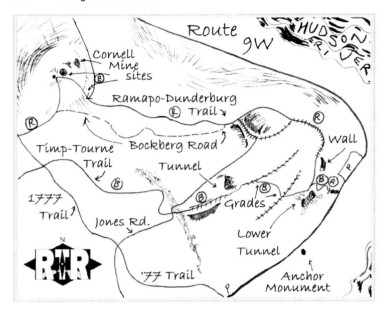

dollars, all there was to show for the laborers' hard work were the astounding constructions that we will discover on this hike. You'll need to bring the Big Flashlight.

The Timp-Torne (blue blaze) and Ramapo-Dunderburg (red blaze) Trails meet Route 9W a few yards south of the sign. Following primarily the blue Timp-Torne Trail, we'll begin our adventure. Minutes in, we'll see a stonework tunnel buried in the woods to the left. This was to have been where the railway cars ended up after the excursion down the mountain (think of it as a carport rather than a tunnel). Investigate the tunnel, and then go back to the T-T and begin climbing in earnest.

This can be a challenging hike. Fortunately, there are numerous rewards for our hard work. Along this section of the trail there are many opportunities to rest and look out high over the Hudson River and across it to the embattled Indian Point nuclear power plant in Buchanan.

In a tough half mile or so from the tunnel, we will begin to see the railway cuts and rights-of-way more clearly. We finally level off at 612 feet and follow a grade to the left (southwesterly). After a few minutes of tracing the old railbed, look to your right—now *that's* what I call a tunnel! Take a minute, break out that flashlight, and do an inspection. This tunnel was supposed to have been cut all the way through the rock but remains unfinished and is frequently mistaken for a cave by those who know less than we do.

Continue southerly on the Timp-Torne for 0.1 miles, admiring the mighty railbed as we go. We now come to a stream crossing and a woods road on the other side. The T-T continues to go straight ahead and up. At this point, before crossing the stream, we can circle around to our right and see the other side of the unfinished tunnel.

Lower tunnel

Upper tunnel

Cross over the water and go to the intersection of the woods road and the T-T. Bear right (northerly) on the unblazed woods road. This is the Jones Trail, actually a service road for the railway during construction. Follow the Jones (unmarked) up, up, up to where it meets with a right-of-way. Turn left (west) and follow the trail through the cut. This is a remarkable section of the railway. If you weren't sure you were following a railbed earlier, you must be sure now. Okay, now step back in time a hundred and ten or so years and imagine you are in an open rail car, gently gliding through this section. The Big City is a hundred miles away . . .

After walking peacefully for a bit, we come across the Ramapo-Dunderburg Trail (red). Bear left (west) and follow it, taking care not to mistakenly take the unmarked woods road that appears on the left a few yards down. That is the Bockberg Road, a woods road that we will encounter again later in the hike.

For now, we leave the scenic spiral railway and start hiking on the R-D towards our next destination, the Cornell iron mine. The trail climbs steadily to the top of Dunderburg Mountain but is gracious enough to pass some high ledges with great views of Bear Mountain, the Hudson River, and the valley below. We'll do the formal tour at the top.

The Cornell Trail (blue) comes in from the right at 0.8 miles after the railbed intersection. Let's start looking for mine sites now. Turning right (north) on the Cornell, there are two mine trenches on the left-hand side of the trail as you descend, identified by tailings piles. Find the first one and about 200 feet lower is the second, also on the left. I include these here only in the spirit of completeness; I'd choose to avoid the steep uphill backtrack, saving my energy for the other Cornell sites, which are more interesting.

At the intersection of the Cornell and Ramapo-Dunderburg is a large exploratory pit. Stay on the R-D, ascending for a short distance until it bears left. Look carefully on your right for a faint path and a cairn, next to a blazed tree (18 T 0584553, 4570851). Follow the level contour of the mountain to your right for about 150 feet, looking for a large tailings pile. Climb the tailings and check out the horizontal tunnel (or adit) of the Cornell Mine (18 T 0584489, 4570871). It's about 5 feet high and usually water-filled. I've seen all sorts of small critters in here and a nest with bird eggs once.

Look above the tunnel slightly to your right and you will see another tailings pile with another mine site worth investigating. These mines were worked sometime around 1859.

Returning to the R-D, climb up to the peak of Bald Mountain, although technically still Dunderburg because there are two summits.

There is a deep vertical shaft near the point where the trail makes a sharp right towards the rocky summit (on the east side of the trail, a few feet downhill). Do check it out with extreme caution. Then get over to the lookout (1,120 feet) and take in that view.

Let us lunch on the rocky top while we survey our domain. To the north is the Bear Mountain Bridge, with Anthony's Nose above the eastern anchorage. There are various stories about this place name, but it is not in honor of the great general "Mad" Anthony Wayne (more about him in the Open Adits chapter). This Anthony apparently was a musician in the Continental army who had a large nose. Follow the bridge to the western side. Just north is Fort Montgomery (new trail there, see the appendix, "Places That Aren't Mentioned in This Book") and south is the site of Fort Clinton, two Revolution-era forts captured by the British in 1777. Do you see the stone tower on top of the mountain straight across the valley? Perkins Memorial Tower sits on top of Bear Mountain. George W. Perkins Sr. was the first chairman of the Palisades Interstate Park Commission, from 1900 to 1920. In the valley below us and slightly forward sits the abandoned hamlet of Doodletown, where we've already hiked, and Iona Island is on the right. To our extreme left (west) is West Mountain. There is a scenic hiking shelter on the south side of West Mountain and an iron mine at the north end.

Continue now on the R-D (in the same direction we've been hiking) for 0.4 miles downhill, where an unmarked woods road comes in on our left. That would be the other end of the Bockberg Road. Take the Bockberg and when in doubt, as the trail occasionally appears to split, stay to the right on the widest path. Don't let that frighten you because it really isn't tough to follow. Take it. We might see ruts in the mud from the park rangers' patrols.

We'll soon return to the junction of Bockberg Road and Ramapo-Dunderburg Trail that we noted earlier today. Bear right (east) on the R-D and follow it all the way back to the parking lot. It climbs through the tall grass for a while before beginning a wild downhill drop, passing endless (thorny) ripe wild raspberry bushes in the summer and equally pervasive wild blueberry bushes, which ripen in the fall.

The R-D was recently relocated to take advantage of the spiral railway grades and we will once more walk on near-completed cuts and features of the rail. Witness the large freestanding cut-stone wall that we walk past. Grades aside, it is the last "new" vestige of the railway that we will come upon today. The R-D joins with the blue Timp-Torne we hiked up earlier and we take the path back downhill (to the left) to Route 9W. Once back at the car, stretch, change out of your hiking shoes, and plan on a hot shower and medication tonight. This was a tough hike!

11

Great Camp Santanoni

WHERE ■ Newcomb, New York

WHY ■ Remains of an abandoned Great Camp in the Adirondacks and primitive campsites beside a lake

DIFFICULTY ■ Moderate, about 10 miles round-trip, with gentle 200-foot elevation change

MAPS ■ Farm site and lodge area maps available (sometimes) at the visitor center in Newcomb

WEB SITE ■ www.aarch.org/html/santanoni/history.html

BROCHURE ■ *A Brief Guide to Camp Santanoni*

UTM COORDINATES
Delia Spring   18 T 0569386, 4874295

DIRECTIONS ■ New York State Thruway (I-87) North to exit 29 (Route 2 West). Take Route 2 West to Route 28N west into Newcomb.

The main lodge of abandoned Camp Santanoni is our primary objective this time out.

Some of the best primitive campsites on the face of the earth are located along Newcomb Lake in the Santanoni Preserve, just before the lodge. I suggest that you take advantage of the camping and do this exploration as a backpacking trip. Bring a good hurricane lamp.

Avoid this hike during black fly season, mid-May to late June; during the day the swarming, tiny, biting monsters will make the trip unbearable as they look for a hot meal at your expense and the equally annoying mosquitoes will snack on you at night.

We will begin with a stop at the Adirondack Visitors Center on Route 28N in Newcomb. Ask for the Camp Santanoni brochure as well as the lodge area and farm site maps, in addition to whatever else they might have regarding the old camp.

Turn left out of the visitor center parking lot (east). There are signs for the Santanoni Preserve parking lot a few miles down on Route 28N. After parking in the upper lot, you will see a trail pointing towards Lake Harris but don't take it. Instead, there is a gated dirt road that we will take up to the camp. Before we do that, though, walk down to the gatehouse, which has a small museum, and start your Great Camp research here. In season, this is where we would find out about tours through the camp.

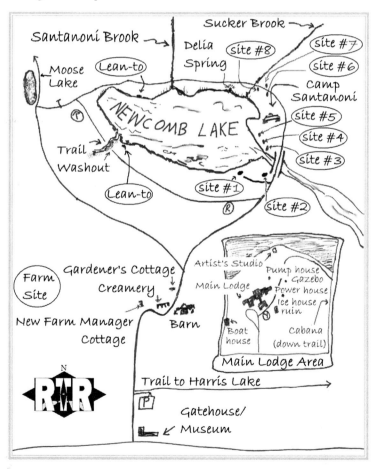

Great Camp Santanoni boathouse

Begin the hike by proceeding north on Newcomb Road (the dirt road), past the trail register. Be sure to sign in. The state gauges trail use that way and it's also a safety issue. The route is clearly signed; the road is wide, mostly level, and easy to follow.

In about a mile we arrive at the farm site, which is our first ruin. As quickly as possible, pull out that farm site map that we scored at the visitors center and let's see what's what. The two most important structures are the huge storybook barn on our right and the stone-arched creamery to the left. (Update: careless smokers caused a fire that destroyed the historic barn in early July 2004.) Incidentally, the last building on the left as we continue our way in is thought to predate the Great Camp period. I've been told the ruin of a maple syrup "sugar house" is a few yards to the left of the path (following a stream uphill) once you cross the first stone bridge past the farm site, but I haven't located that particular structure yet. At 2.5 miles, a trail comes in on the left. It heads through the woods another 5 or so miles towards Moose Pond, where a boathouse once existed.

The hiking is easy as we make our way to the old camp. A red trail appears on our left as we close in. That trail circles Newcomb Lake and accesses the first of two lean-tos; the other is off the yellow trail that intersects with the red on the other side of the lake. There is a hiker's bridge washout at the far end of the lake. To get from one side of the red trail to the other requires removing shoes and socks to cross the brook.

There are eight primitive campsites dotted along the eastern side of Newcomb Lake, and let's not forget the two lean-tos flanking the lake further west. Closer to the camp itself, campsites #1 and #5 are the pick, in my opinion. Site #1 is the most remote and has an outhouse, but no picnic table. It also has a small sandy beach on the lakeshore. Nice! Sites #3, #4, and #5 have outhouses and picnic tables, are roomy, and are nicely isolated from the world. Site #8 is a large group site. I can't prove this but I suspect that some of the folks that are currently working at Santanoni have held some pretty good parties at this one (the makeshift bar I saw there is the tip-off). The other sites (#2, #6, and #7) are less attractive and are right off the hiking trail that circles the lake, thereby affording little sense of privacy in their isolation. Sometimes picnic tables are there but on my last visit there weren't any tables at sites #6 or #7.

Before we properly explore the Great Camp, let's drop our packs at site #2 and have lunch beside the lake. Fueled and ready, it's time to cross over the wooden bridge and head down the road towards Great Camp Santanoni.

We don't see the big house until we are right on top of it. I'll withhold a detailed description because the initial discovery is the key to a proper first impression.

This is a magnificent place. On the other side of the house is a flight of steps leading downhill to a small clearing that affords a wide view of the calm lake and cloud-ringed mountains that surround it. The artist's studio, just to the right of the main building, has expansive views of Newcomb Lake through wide, arched windows. The remains of a large boathouse are to the left of the lodge and some other fallen buildings lie near the main yellow trail that cuts through the site. The remnants of a cabana sit beside a small beach just down the trail, past the lodge and before the last few campsites.

Delia Spring, with its supposed restorative qualities, supplied water to the main house via pipeline from its location on the north shore of Newcomb Lake about a quarter mile past Sucker Brook. The spring is far easier to locate by boat from the lake: just look for the pipe leading downhill with the magical spring water bubbling up in a miniature geyser from the end of the pipe, just above the water level. Whenever I mentioned to locals that I was looking for Delia Spring (18 T 0569386, 4874295), they all wished me luck finding the Fountain of Youth.

The first time I came here was during a spring 2002 backpacking trip with a friend. It was a miserably raw, cold, wet day and most of it was spent establishing our campsite. It wasn't until nighttime that we were first able to explore the main house. He had a flashlight and I

**Back
of the lodge**

used a small Dietz Comet hurricane lamp. We were able to go into
some unlocked rooms and used only the flickering lamplight to navigate through the lodge. This is good stuff.

The big house is quiet, lonely, and elegant after dark, not menac-
ing at all. It may not fully understand why someone would want to
abandon it. The reason is best told around our campfire tonight.

The 1890s were the beginning of a time when wealthy families
built Adirondack Great Camps, which are large, rustic-style vacation
estates. White Pine Camp and Camp Sagamore are two of the better-
known camps and both are open for tours in the summer. Over thirty
of these Great Camps were known to have existed. Robert Pruyn (pronounced "prine") was a well-connected Albany businessman who had
amassed close to thirteen thousand acres near Newcomb. He began
building Camp Santanoni in 1892 and completed it by the following
year. It was among the first of these Great Camps and architecturally it
was probably the most highly regarded. At the peak of its existence,

Camp Santanoni was entirely self-supporting by way of a large farm that provided meat, milk, and greens, and the surplus was sold in local area markets.

Camp Santanoni does not have the huge buildings or bowling alleys sometimes associated with Great Camps, such as Sagamore. What it does have is its own unique style. There are many differently designed groups of buildings that survived the abandonment. The six-bedroom gatehouse has a classical stone arch entrance. The farm complex site is notable for its expansive size, native stone buildings, and a European look until thoughtless fools torched the barn. The main lodge is actually six separate buildings with a common roof and porch done in Adirondack rustic style. When seen from above, the roofline suggests a symbolic Phoenix in flight, which was an influence from the days when Robert's father was U.S. ambassador to Japan, from 1862 to 1865 under Abraham Lincoln.

The Melvin family of Syracuse bought Camp Santanoni in 1953. They lived and played there into the 1970s, on a somewhat reduced grand scale. In 1971, their eight-year-old cousin Douglas Legg and his father were walking through the property when Douglas was told to go back to the house and put on long pants for poison ivy protection (there is no poison ivy in the Adirondacks). The young man disappeared on his way back to the lodge and was never seen again. A massive manhunt lasting over a week was launched in a frantic attempt to locate him but no trace was ever found.

Porch in back of lodge

Devastated by this tragic event, the Melvins sold the camp and it eventually became state property through various land deals. Except for occasional hunters or campers staying overnight, the old camp has stood vacant and abandoned in the woods since that time.

Camp Santanoni became part of the New York State Forest Preserve in 1972. Most of the original estate had become part of the High Peaks Wilderness Area, while the rest went to the Vanderwacker Mountain Wild Forest. In 2000, the Camp Santanoni Historic Area was created to protect thirty-two acres of the old camp, the farm site, and the road in. It is also a National Historic Landmark as of 2000.

Presently there is a restoration project going on and occasional guided tours will go through the lodge. During the summer you can take a horse-drawn wagon into Camp Santanoni. Some people put their canoes on the wagon and use them on Newcomb Lake. It can be a busy place, with hikers, bikers, canoers, and day-trippers on horse-pulled wagons all sharing the road on the way to explore Santanoni.

Tonight, however, we're camping beside the lake and after the day people leave we have this tranquil wooded place all to ourselves. We can build our campfire and cook a nice dinner while we drink the water we bottled earlier today from the Fountain of Youth. After dark we'll let the fire burn down, grab our hurricane lamps, and then go out and explore the place again . . .

12

Hasenclever Iron Trail

WHERE ▪ Long Pond Ironworks State Park, New Jersey

WHY ▪ Many ruins at Long Pond Ironworks State Park; Peter's, Hope, and Patterson Mine sites

DISTANCE ▪ Moderate, about 8 miles round-trip with some hills

MAP ▪ New York–New Jersey Trail Conference map 100, Sterling Forest Trails; area topographic map.

PAMPHLET ▪ *Welcome to the Hasenclever Iron Trail*

WEB SITES ▪ www.longpondironworks.org, www.toxiclegacy.com, www.epa.gov/superfund (search Peter's Mine)

CONTACT ▪ Friends of Long Pond Ironworks, P.O. Box 809, Hewitt, NJ 07421; 973-657-1688

UTM COORDINATES
Unmarked road at Sterling Ridge Trail 18 T 0558933, 4555889
Unmarked road junction 18 T 0558925, 4555688
Unmarked road and Hasenclever Trail 18 T 0558394, 4556383
Hope Mine 1 18 T 0561748, 4555666
Hope Mine 2 18 T 0561732, 4555614
Hope Mine 3 18 T 0561710, 4555562
Hope Mine 4 18 T 0561659, 4555527

DIRECTIONS ▪ New York State Thruway (I-87) North to exit 15, Route 17 North. Take 17 North about 1.25 miles to the turnoff for Route 72 and Sterling Forest. Follow the road past Sterling Forest and the Ringwood sites and make a right on Margaret King Avenue, then another right on Route 511. Take 511 for just over a mile and park by the old store in Hewitt, New Jersey, now the Long Pond Ironworks Museum.

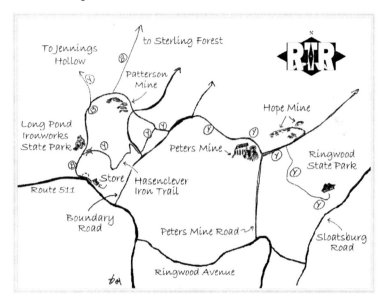

The newly marked Hasenclever Iron Trail (2004) goes from Long Pond Ironworks to Ringwood State Park, tracing the historic route of Ramapo iron ore from mine to furnace to ironmaster.

The historic district around Long Pond Ironworks and Ringwood State Park, including Sterling Forest to the north, is riddled with over fifty mine sites of various sizes and was the heart of iron mining in the region for nearly two hundred years. Many of those mine sites are filled in or have otherwise faded from view. Some of the iron-making furnaces from the period still remain within close range: here at Long Pond, the Wawayanda furnace in the eponymous state park, the Clinton furnace near the eponymous reservoir, and the remarkably intact Southfields furnace by Bramertown Road and Orange Turnpike (Route 19), near Sterling Forest in New York, are just a few that come to mind.

Peter Hasenclever arrived in America from Germany, by way of England, in October 1764 and quickly bought the decaying Ringwood Ironworks for five thousand pounds sterling from the Ogden family, who had established the furnaces about twenty years before. He had big plans for his new ironworks and went about adding other similar properties to his new empire. The spending spree alarmed his European partners in their "American (or London) Company" as more properties were acquired and as mining began and furnaces were built under his stewardship. Returning to London in November 1766, he met with some new associates in the company and convinced them to keep moving ahead with his plan. Returning to the Ramapo Mountains in 1767 with a fresh contract, he had seemingly convinced his partners that additional investment would reap huge rewards due to the massive amounts of iron ore in their present assets and projected future properties.

His return to the ironworks, however, was distressing. The construction of furnaces and other works had not only stopped but existing structures were in a state of decay. If that wasn't bad enough, a month and a half later, one Jeston Humfray, representing the American Company back in England, arrived and relieved Hasenclever of his duties as ironmaster despite the agreement forged in England. His partners had mysteriously changed their minds. Hasenclever initiated legal maneuverings, attacking his successor and asserting his own rightful place as the man in charge, but he never regained control of the empire he had so grandly envisioned.

While posthumous credit is given to Peter Hasenclever for his vision in recognizing the iron-making potential of the region, poor cash management skills destroyed his dream in the end. He died a successful businessman, however, in Germany in 1793.

Hasenclever Iron Trail

Robert Erskine entered the picture in 1771, becoming ironmaster four years after Hasenclever was fired. During the Revolution he sided with the colonists, becoming a captain and surveyor in the Continental army. Other notable ironmasters with famous names like Martin Ryerson and Cooper Hewitt & Co. closed out the iron-making years at Ringwood, but a few of their mines still lie buried off hiking trails that we are getting to know very well.

Regarding today's adventure, this can be an intense exploration dealing with a network of unmarked roads and poking around the wild Peter's Mine complex, in its day one of this area's major iron producers up to the 1930s. Added into the mix are the Ramapough Mountain People, descendants of mine workers who are part African American, Spanish, Dutch, and Native American and live around the Peter's Mine site. They are known to have intimidated hikers and mine explorers in the past. Things are supposed to be different these days.

The best way to do this hike is to first take the guided tour of the Long Pond Ironworks site, conducted from March through October by volunteers. Find out the times offered by checking out www.long-pondironworks.org. The guides take us around the extensive ruins and expertly interpret them, giving us useful knowledge for the day's adventures. Long Pond State Park features two waterwheels, plenty of historic homes in various interesting states of decay, an uncompleted giant waterwheel foundation, and a general store ruin, among other items we've gone to a lot of trouble to seek out over these adventures. Once we tell our guide we're following this book, we'll be treated like we're Hasenclever himself! The earliest tour is usually at 10 A.M., so we should plan on taking it so we can start our hike afterwards at about 11. This can be a lengthy day of walking and exploring, so a long mid-summer day might be the best time to do it. Expect to spend close to an hour just photographing Peter's Mine. Before we set out, let's be sure to grab a copy of the *Welcome to the Hasenclever Iron Trail* pamphlet, available at Ringwood State Park and also at the Long Pond Ironworks Museum.

Another thing we'll need to do is obtain a topographical map of the area we plan to explore, which is the route of the trail between Long Pond Ironworks and Ringwood State Park. Topozone.com is a good resource. The vicinity is laced with unmarked trails and mining roads, which can be confusing, to say the least. The unmarked trails and roads are both indicated as dotted lines on the Trail Conference map, but are distinguished differently on the topographical, which is why we need both sources for successful navigation.

An additional fly in the ointment is the vast amount of magnetic iron in the surrounding hills, at times causing misleading compass

Dynamite shed

readings. New York State actually benefited from the compass errors, gaining land when early map makers made mistakes while surveying the state line following false readings. I'm mighty glad the Road to Ruins Investigation Team had the GPS to let us know when we were on the wrong path. GPS sure is the dopey hikers' friend!

The day's planned route is to take the blue Sterling Ridge Trail (also the Highlands Trail, which will one day link existing trails into a long-distance pathway in New Jersey) north to the Patterson Mine, then generally east on an unmarked road over to the Hope and Peter's Mines, returning to Long Pond on the yellow-blazed Hasenclever Iron Trail. You could do this trip in reverse, that is, starting off on the Hasenclever but I think it's harder to find the Patterson Mine going that way. It would be great if the mine road could be blazed into a trail for easier navigation between the sites.

All right then. We've just finished the tour and we're heading northward on the blue Sterling Ridge Trail. As we cross over the wooden bridge just east of the furnace site, we'll notice yellow blazes bearing to the right (east). That would be the Hasenclever Trail but we'll pick up the other end of it on the way home. Following blue for 1.1 miles, passing along the way the yellow Jennings Hollow Trail (where a minor farm ruin sits), an unmarked road splits from the Sterling Ridge Trail (at 18 T 558394, 4556383) and heads to the right (east). The Patterson Mine (18 T 558692, 4556258) sits 0.2 miles east of the intersection, consisting of three deep pits and their tailings piles around the trail and a small test pit at the western end.

The mine can be traced back to 1870, with all activity ending about 1903. George Patterson bought a home on Greenwood Turnpike and the 240 acres of land surrounding it, including the mine, in 1842. In the 1980s, his house was moved to Long Pond Ironworks in preparation for the creation of Monksville Reservoir, which isn't represented on maps made from the NAD27 (North American Datum 1927) survey. Mostly a test site, ore was never shipped from the Patterson Mine.

When we've finished our investigations, be sure to return to the mine road we came from; there is a trail leading from the western end of the mine that heads south and it's easy to take it by mistake. Navigation becomes a challenge on the next part of this trip. Continuing southeasterly for 0.3 miles brings us to an intersection with another unmarked road (18 T 0558933, 4555889) where we'll bear to the left (northeast) and trudge up about sixty yards before again turning to the right (southeast), blessedly connecting with the yellow Hasenclever Iron Trail (at 18 T 055925, 4555688) after a walk of 0.2 miles. It's a relief to hit a marked trail.

The yellow blazes continue on past more exasperatingly unmarked roads for just under 2 miles to the Peter's Mine site. We know we're getting close when signs of civilization, AKA trash, begin to appear. A hunter's platform high in a tree, discarded tires, makeshift chairs and tables, and other detritus mark the vicinity as accurately as a GPS waypoint might. When the RTR Investigation Team took a quick lunch break just before getting to the mine, we heard a loud motor vehicle crashing through the woods behind us on the trail we just took, but we never saw anyone.

We've certainly seen our share of mines and ruins on these hikes, but Peter's Mine is in a class by itself. Thorough investigation will bring us past 1940s-era mining remains, much newer than we're used to. This isn't a mere hole in the ground or flooded shaft. Extreme caution must be used when nosing around because there are more than a few high drops onto hard rock below, so there is no room for a mistake.

The Ramapough People's reputation for threatening behavior and vehicle vandalism is well known and local State Park representatives and historians consulted with them as the trail was being planned. Whatever agreement was reached, they still live right next to the mine and respect for their property is important.

When I began to research this book, my first visit to the Peter's Mine site came towards the middle of my investigations. I knew nothing of the Ramapough People. I parked my car at the barrier at the end of Peter's Mine Road, put my backpack on, and began my hike. I was alone on this exploration. A few steps in, I looked to my left and saw what appeared to be the mine on the other side of a junk yard.

Walking toward the mine, I approached a hill with mine relics clearly visible ahead. I continued on but saw that a person dressed in hunter's camouflage from head to toe was standing at the top of the hill, facing me. I decided to keep going despite his steady staredown. When I reached him, I noticed shacks, rabbit hutches, and chicken coops down a hill to my left. What in the world was going on here?

I asked him, "Is this private property?"

"No," was all he said.

"Is this Peter's Mine?"

"Yes."

The cold glare and one-word answers were all I received but I kept on pressing him. In a little while, he warmed up. I found out his name was Matt, he was in his twenties, and he was one of the Ramapough People. He took me on a guided insider's tour of the mine complex. He showed me shafts that we accessed by walking through their property, something most people (myself included) would never do by themselves. It was a fascinating experience and I'm lucky I did it.

Because of the danger, I will not reveal where a major shaft goes diagonally down into the depths of the hillside but I will give a clue to where it is. If you stand in the filled-in main shaft depression and look up at the hillside, you might see where the opening comes to the surface. You need to climb down a sheer cliffside to get to it. No one in their right mind would do this if one didn't know it was there. I'll repeat that there is no room for error when exploring this site.

The state of New Jersey has been trying to get the Ramapoughs to leave the mine site for years, but there is unwillingness among them to do that. What makes this story compelling is that illegal dumping of toxic materials, pollution caused by chemicals that are used in mining, plus the fact that the Ford Motor Company used the site as a dumping ground for lead paint in the mid-1960s, creating a Superfund site in the 1970s, are slowly killing the people living around it. Asthma, cancers, and other nasty illnesses have been inflicted on virtually everyone living around the mine, yet still they refuse to sell. This complex issue is better explained at www.toxiclegacy.com.

The first artifacts we come across as we hike the yellow trail are circular concrete "tailing thickener" tanks, as identified in *Iron Mine Trails*. The filled-in mine shaft opening is in the clearing beyond the tanks, and the ore-processing plant is behind the clearing, on a hill. This mine once extended some 2,400 feet and seventeen levels down into the earth, second only to the Forest of Dean Mine (now on West Point property and completely covered over) in size and production.

Peter's Mine ore concentrator

Climbing up the black earth embankment next to the ore-processing plant, we can look carefully around. There is much to see and photograph here, but the roof has many holes and I can't say how safe it is. Watch your footing.

Continuing on a path uphill, the deep pit that was a rock crusher (or ore concentrator) is the last major structure up here. Identify it by the poured-concrete wall with a door opening under massive steel beams. It's awful scary peeking inside. That's a mighty long drop onto the unforgiving rock far below on the other side of the door.

Notice the other door all the way at the bottom. The steel framework, rusting over the years, stretches across the chasm. Awesome. This is one place where you definitely do not want someone you don't know in back of you.

Are we done with Peter's Mine? If so, heading north on the Hasenclever Iron Trail will bring us to the next mine site, the Hope Mine. The trail joins with a service road for a short time. The Hasenclever Trail will leave Peter's Mine Road as it heads easterly to Ringwood but we'll stay on the service road (north) for 0.2 miles.

The Hope Mine complex is on our left at that point. Approaching the Hope Mine road, the RTR Investigation Team was warned by a group of camo-clad, gun-toting Ramapough hunters that other armed hunters were coming over the hillside and it wasn't safe for us to go up there. We thanked them and left the area, but returned a half hour later because we figured they were just trying to get rid of us and there weren't any other hunters. We didn't meet up with any. Maybe they didn't want us to scare any game away. Maybe they still don't like hikers.

An old mine road accesses the site, and you've almost certainly noticed the tailings piles already. Up the hill, about 300 feet in, is the main Hope Mine opening, a massive flooded shaft with the remains of a fence surrounding it. This place is super dangerous. Beware of soft-shouldered steep drops into the toxic flooded mine shaft (18 T 0561748, 4555666). Follow the old mine road uphill (southwesterly) to the next cut (18 T 0561732, 4555614).

The last two cuts, both worthwhile to seek out, are found by picking our way (still southwesterly) up the old road. They're about 250 feet apart from each other (18 T 0561710, 4555562 and 18 T 0561659, 4555527).

When we are finished with the Hope Mine, returning to the Hasenclever Iron Trail and following it back in a southwesterly direction will bring us back to Long Pond Ironworks in about an hour and a half. Numbers posted on trees point out historic sites interpreted by the trail brochure we picked up in the morning.

There is an element of danger on this hike that the others don't have. It was exciting and unique, but I have to admit I'm glad it's over.

Update (spring 2006): Since clumps of lead paint and toxic sludge are repeatedly being discovered in area people's lawns, the Peter's Mine site is about to become the first relisted Superfund site in the history of the program. The continuity of the Hasenclever Trail will be interrupted during this latest cleanup and it will not be relocated.

13
Island Pond Ranger Cabin

WHERE ▪ At the end of unmarked Island Pond Road in Harriman State Park, New York

WHY ▪ Ruins of a ranger cabin on a lake, two mines, plus a historic park shelter

DIFFICULTY ▪ Easy, about 5 miles round-trip, one short but steep climb

MAPS ▪ New York–New Jersey Trail Conference map 4, Harriman/Bear Mountain Trails

DIRECTIONS ▪ Palisades Parkway North to exit 14. Make a right onto Route 98, which becomes Route 106. We begin at the parking area on Route 106, about 1.5 miles west of the intersection of Route 106 and Seven Lakes Drive. There are a few parking pullouts in the vicinity but the one we want has the White Bar Trail (white-blazed) crossing the road nearby.

This is a good hike for beginners or families with young children because the terrain has minimal elevation changes, except for the path up to the shelter. The features we're looking for are close to each other and visually impressive.

We'll start out by picking up the White Bar Trail and following it north. The WB and unmarked Island Pond road will soon join together for a short time. The WB bears right after a few minutes of walking but we will stay to the left on unblazed Island Pond Road.

This is a wild, attractive part of the park and this section makes for pleasant, mostly level hiking except for the rise on the way up to the shelter later on. At 0.75 miles from the car, turn right (east) on the yellow-blazed Dunning Trail. In a few yards you will encounter the dark Boston Mine, a cut in the hillside to the left of the trail. Walk through the cut ahead of you and look around to see the actual mine shaft, now flooded. It is thought to have been active around 1880, mining magnetite iron. This is a fine mine site and a good warm-up for the ranger cabin ruin.

Once you are back on Island Pond Road, continue heading north, straight past the Arden-Surebridge Trail (red-blazed) to the ruin of the ranger cabin. The Garfield Mine lurks off a left-hand spur trail just before you reach the old parking area for the cabin. The Garfield is a series of uninteresting Parrott Brothers exploratory trenches (see the Mines! All Mines! chapter for more on them) from around 1880, usually filled with water and a bit tricky to identify as a mine.

The cabin ruin sits at the south tip of scenic Island Pond and was built for park rangers to party and entertain sometime around the 1920s. In 1963, idiotic vandals playing with matches destroyed it. The stone foundation, the chimney, and some walls are all that's left. It is an entertaining task trying to picture what the cabin looked like but clearly it was an attractive building in an exceptionally picturesque setting.

This will be our lunch spot. After lunch, suit up and we'll retrace our steps on Island Pond Road (south) back to the yellow Dunning Trail. Turn left onto Dunning (east) and follow it up and down through the woods, passing the Boston Mine and the White Bar Trail (they run

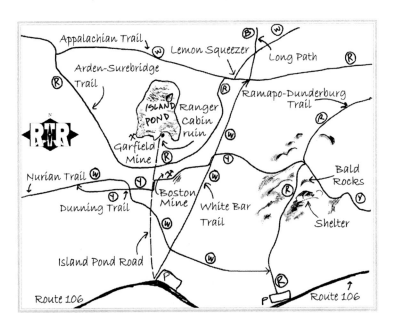

together for 0.15 miles), eventually reaching the red-on-white-blazed Ramapo-Dunderburg Trail.

Follow the R-D to the right (south) as it climbs up a rocky ridge and peaks out at 1,382 feet. Traveling south, at 0.2 miles from the intersection you will soon encounter the Bald Rock Shelter, built in 1933 with stone taken from the immediate area. Backpackers can hike to these shelters and stay overnight, first come, first served. The shel-

Boston Mine

Cabin ruin

Ranger cabin

ters are open in the front and do little to protect you against bugs, critters, or serious weather. Personally, I'd rather sleep in a tent at night.

There is a network of these shelters scattered throughout the park, usually taking advantage of high viewpoints. The Civilian Conservation Corps built them, mostly during the 1930s. In fact, to digress a moment, Harriman State Park itself owes much to Roosevelt's New Deal. The roads through the park, landscaping, construction of shelters and buildings, damming of lakes, and place names all stem from this period.

These shelters make excellent day hike destinations in their own right. Some have fireplaces that are suitable for cooking. (Tip: Gather up some firewood or bring match-light charcoal and burn a burger up there.) People leave all sorts of things in these shelters, such as books, cans of food, and sometimes cooking grills.

Continuing south on the R-D, bear right when you reach the Nurian Trail (white), at 0.75 miles south of the shelter. Once you reach the White Bar Trail at about 0.4 miles, turn left (south) and follow it back to the parking area. Quite a lovely little loop we just did!

14
Mines! All Mines!

WHERE ▪ Harriman State Park, New York

WHY ▪ Multiple old iron mines, historic shelter, forest fire site, Times Square of the woods

DIFFICULTY ▪ Challenging, 8 miles with significant elevation changes

MAP ▪ New York–New Jersey Trail Conference map 4, Northern Harriman Trails

UTM COORDINATES
Hogencamp Mine   18 T 0573780, 4566182
Pine Swamp Mine   18 T 0574269, 4566805

DIRECTIONS ▪ New York State Thruway (I-87) to exit 15A, Route 17 North. Continue to Seven Lakes Drive and turn right, into the park. Take Seven Lakes Drive towards Bear Mountain and park at the lot on Lake Skannatati, 0.7 miles north of the Kanawauke Circle.

Harriman State Park is truly a great destination for us ruin-hunters. Iron mines, historic shelters, old cemeteries, and more await our explorations in just about all the different areas of this park. Unmarked woods roads, arteries to long-vanished farms and mines, lace the park. Beside all that, it is a very attractive park with many different variations in landscape as you hike from one section to the next. On this tour we will check out a few iron mines and also Times Square, a well-known trail junction where several paths intersect. When hiking in this section, you can't help but cross it at least once. You should bring the Big Flashlight on this trip.

After parking the car, locate the red-triangle-blazed Arden-Surebridge (A-SB) Trail and follow it westerly and uphill, leaving behind the citizens who hang around the lake as we climb up to Pine Swamp Mountain. After hiking for a short time, our first reward is a fine 1,125-foot viewpoint overlooking the lake with clear views to the southwest. The A-SB undulates up and down for another 0.45 miles and soon gets interesting.

Passing through the second of two low-lying hemlock groves we'll encounter, it's time to start looking down. At the end of the hemlocks the trail goes up and doglegs to the left as we pick up the old mine road (still the Arden-Surebridge Trail). Just before the left turn are some noteworthy glacial erratics but what we came to see is some iron ore. It's scattered all around us in great rusted quantities. Whip out your magnetometer (or a compass if you only have that) and start reading some rocks. Some of their iron content is magnetic and will have an effect on a compass needle.

I've frequently impressed the girls by picking up iron ore chunks and breaking off nice big pieces (with an appropriate accompanying grunt), easily accomplished due to the oxidation of the iron (but they sure didn't know *that*!). Iron ore is normally a slate gray but becomes red-streaked and flaky as it rusts, so follow the trail of rusted iron up to the road and start looking around.

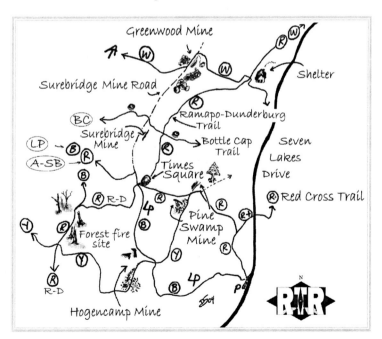

Pine Swamp
Mine

Mine pits are scattered around the trail and there is an impressive horizontal cut on the right side of the trail just before we approach a wide stream. Let's cross over and then pick up the yellow-blazed Dunning Trail, heading left (southwesterly). Pine Swamp is now clearly presented on our left. Follow Dunning down a short distance to where we see a cleft (usually with a stream running through, passing under the trail in a culvert) in the hillside on our right. If we begin to follow the stream uphill, before we get very far we can see a mine cut on the left (south) side of the stream. It's a warm-up for things to come.

To find the Pine Swamp Mine, continue along the yellow Dunning (which also passes the Boston Mine in another hike) for about 60 yards until we see a faint trail by a yellow-blazed tree. It leads sharply uphill past familiar black tailings to a clearing, with the main mine opening just a few feet in (18 T 0574269, 4566805).

The Pine Swamp Mine is exciting. A Parrott Brothers acquisition, this mine was worked from 1830 off and on until 1880. The shaft runs over 100 feet along a diagonal vein and the walls of the tunnel are about 40 feet high in some places. I've heard it compared to a subway tunnel. There is an opening in the roof at the far end, where sunlight comes through on a clear day, emphasizing the sheer volume of the excavation. It is possible to walk from one end to the other but be advised that signs on the site declare it off limits. The ore vein that was being mined continues below the mine entrance into an area that is now flooded. After exploring the mine area, exit back out to the level area just outside the mine. Head to the left (north), following the remains of old roads that circled through. They lead to other cuts and shafts of the mine, and an odd iron eyelet protruding from the top of a boulder.

Robert and Peter Parrott owned iron mines and foundries in the area and needed all the ore they could get their hands on. Their innovation in the world of nineteenth-century munitions was the rifled-bore and banded cannon barrel. The rifled bore shot ordinance out with a spin (think of a football in flight), improving distance and accuracy. The banded barrel had external iron bands wrapped around the cannon. The bands increased the strength of the cannon by preventing ruptures upon firing and also allowed quicker breech (rear) loading. The Parrott brothers didn't invent these improvements but were able to develop reliable manufacturing processes, especially the secure placing of the iron bands. Foundries owned by the Parrotts produced many different cast iron finished goods, but weapons were foremost. The West Point Foundry area that we will hike in another chapter was also a Parrott operation.

Once we're done exploring the mine area, return to the yellow Dunning Trail. The Dunning is a wide, mostly level woods road at this point as we skirt the swamp and head south. Pass by the Long Path (turquoise blue–blazed), continue straight ahead for a few yards, and then look around. This is the site of the 1870–1885 Hogencamp Mine (18 T 0573780, 4566182 puts us in the middle of the complex); a series of open trench cuts are visible on the right side (west) of the trail. There are six mine trenches to discover, some foundations, cuts, pits, and an impressive opening into the hillside. It doesn't have one spectacular shaft like the Pine Swamp Mine but pound-for-pound has possibly the greatest concentration of relics of any mine site in this park. Various sources note the site of a village along the Long Path, northwest of the Dunning junction and above the mine site.

Follow the tailings piles and all will be revealed. Most notable is the high, deep-slotted mine cut that appears to tunnel under the Long Path as that trail heads up and over the mine site on its way to Times Square. A piece of rebar sticking up out of the rock (part of a safety barrier, one would think) identifies the cut from the Long Path.

As we continue along on the Dunning, the forest changes from swamp to drier ground as the elevation rises. Trees give way to large open expanses of rock faces and domes. As we approach the red Ramapo-Dunderburg Trail, it becomes apparent that there was a forest fire here. In fact, sometime during the mid-1980s, a fire came through here and did acres of damage. It remains interesting to see how the recovery process continues. Baby pines are everywhere, as are bleached and burnt trunks of probably second-growth pine.

Warning: The intersection of the yellow Dunning and red Ramapo-Dunderburg is easy to miss. Be attentive and read your topo carefully. We've missed the R-D if we go through the open rocky section, descend on the Dunning, and then reenter a thickly wooded area.

With Hogencamp Mountain looming on our right (easterly), pick up the R-D and take it to the right, northeasterly. This is a very primal-looking part of the park, with burnt forest, rocks and boulders of all sizes strewn around, and few healthy mature trees. Sharp, white trunks of pine trees killed in the fire of the mid-1980s cover the hillsides as far as we can see, spiking skyward. Just think back to what the Pine Swamp area looked like. We'll do some climbing up large, open rock faces as we make our way up to Ship Rock, supposedly so named due to the fact that it resembles (to some trailblazers) the upended hull of a ship. Okay, if they say so. To me it looks like a big stone hill. On a hot summer day, the reflected heat from the bare rocks can be intense. More rock hopping will eventually lead us down to the famous trail junction known as Times Square.

A stone fireplace marks Times Square, as does a large glacial erratic with the various trails named and "arrowed" to point the way. Three different blazed trails meet here and to the north is the unmarked Surebridge Mine Road. The Long Path (LP) and Arden-Surebridge (A-SB) Trails meet the Ramapo-Dunderburg (R-D) Trail at this point. Go left (north) on the LP/A-SB Trails and shortly they both bend to the left. A wide woods road is now before us: the Surebridge Mine Road.

We have an easy, mostly level half mile or so on Surebridge Mine Road until we approach our next iron mine. The Surebridge Mine appears on our right just before an intersection with the Bottle Cap Trail (blazed with white bottle caps).

Beginning in 1880, this mine produced some 458 tons of iron ore for its owners, the Parrott Brothers. The Surebridge Mine has the unmistakable feeling of industrial activity in years past. The site is generally a series of cuts, trenches, pits, rock piles, and flooded shafts that scar the landscape endlessly, some features being revealed by a little off-trail poking around. It is interesting to explore this area with or

Eyebolt in rock

without other references. There are no enterable shafts (or adits) at this mine.

Continuing down the mine road for another half mile, our last iron mine of the day is on our right, just before the old road meets the Appalachian Trail. The 1838-era Greenwood Mine was yet another Parrott iron mine, with ore shipping to the various Parrott holdings. There is a 100-foot flooded trench just beside the road. Tailings piles, flooded pits, and variously shaped cuts are all within easy exploration

Greenwood Mine

radius. By keeping our eyes open we can locate the road that leads uphill to the main mine shaft, which is also flooded.

Our next move is to take the Appalachian Trail to the right (east) up Fingerboard Mountain to the shelter there (notice we join the R-D Trail along the way). The Fingerboard Shelter (1928) sits at 1,300 feet, with Lake Tioratti below us and to the east. This is a comfortable spot to eat lunch or just take a break.

Leaving the AT, we'll take the R-D south (we took it north earlier today) down Fingerboard Mountain and back to Times Square. Pick up the turquoise blue–blazed Long Path (which runs from the George Washington Bridge to Whiteface Mountain in the Adirondacks) and follow it to the left (south) over Pine Swamp Mountain and back to the car. Although we explored a good number of interesting Harriman mines on this little excursion, our appetite for old iron has only been whetted for future adventures.

15
Mount Hope Historical Park

WHERE   Mount Hope, New Jersey

WHY   Extensive mining artifacts and ruins

DIFFICULTY   Easy, 3–4 miles, minor elevation changes

MAPS   Mount Hope Historical Park and Morris County Parks Commission maps

DIRECTIONS   I-80 West to exit 35, Mount Hope Avenue. After 0.5 miles, turn left onto Richard Mine Road and then turn right after 0.7 miles onto Coburn Road (turns into Teabo Road). The park entrance is on our left 0.7 miles from the turn. The way to the park is well signed from the interstate exit.

This small park has the greatest concentration of ruins and mine pits in this book. Although the hiking is actually minimal, budget a good three and a half hours or so for proper exploration. There are many side trails that are hard to ignore.

After parking, locate the kiosk with maps at the eastern end of the lot and read the historical information posted on the board. It tells us that mining began at the Mount Hope sites in about 1772 and continued until 1958. The largest workings were known as the Richard, Teabo, and Allen Mines. These three different veins of magnetite iron ore were all mined on this site, with the earliest known commercial mining occurring around 1820. Rockaway Township mines produced about 50 percent of all of New Jersey's iron during the eighteenth century.

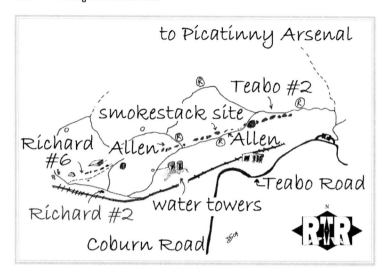

Let's follow the trail up from the lot to a point where it splits into a red-blazed trail bearing left, and white- and blue-blazed trails bearing to the right. More on the white and blue trails later on. We'll take the red trail up the hill.

After about fifteen minutes of walking from the parking lot, the trail turns sharply left at a sign that warns:

No Hiking
Federal Government Property
Turn Around To Continue Hiking

If we ignore the sign and continue straight, we'll come up on the grounds of the Picatinny Arsenal, where Uncle Sam devises advanced weapons for the military. Not a good place to sneak up on! Besides, we've noticed that the diggings and pits have begun so let's respect the warning on the sign and continue with the red trail.

The mine pits are now coming fast and furious as we hike on. We soon see a post with a number 4 on it, which corresponds to a historical narrative on the back of the map. This would be Teabo #2, worked from 1880 to 1883. The Teabo Mine was one of the three major mines on this property.

Continuing on the trail, we'll soon come to a split where red branches off red. Stay to the left and post #5 comes up, the Allen Mine site, named for Jabez Allen, who was the property owner between 1848 and 1868. Numerous trenches and pits litter the area, following the Richard ore vein. The Allen tunnel and smoke stack sites are just ahead at marker #6. In 1855, the tunnel ran 600 feet from Teabo Road (outside the park) into the ore body and was the main access into the Allen Mine. No visible remains of either the tunnel or the stack are extant here.

Yes, there sure are plenty of holes in the ground around here. We're both hoping things get a bit more interesting, right?

In a short time we come to another trail split, this time an orange trail branching off from red. Bear right on the red trail, and then left in a short time onto the other end of the orange trail (red heads off to the right). There are a few trenches and pits along the trail in this section and a few mysterious vent pipes poking out of the ground. What are they venting? How do we get to it?

Soon enough, after hiking for about twenty minutes or so, we pass unmarked spurs that veer off to points unknown. One heads off toward a group of houses. A broken brick pillar becomes visible on the right-hand side of the trail, a sign that some good discoveries are coming up soon. Point #7, the Richard Mine and Richard 6, an 1897 shaft, soon present themselves. Both operations worked parts of the Richard vein. Right around this post we will see a concrete trapezoidal structure up the hill on our left. We will now begin our explorations in earnest.

Bushwhacking up to the trapezoid, as we look around several mine structures will come into view. There is a concrete platform nearby with iron rods at the far end. Steel cables lie about and a bent water pipe is just behind it. Near the ground there is an iron ring set into the vertical far corner of the concrete pad. Several coils of steel cable are here, too. We can see the open corner remains of a building

Mount Hope Historical Park

across the way. Climb up a bit and a faint trail becomes visible. It is indicated by a dotted line on the park map. Note that it is not the bold dotted line at post #8. Keep climbing. Deep trenches are on our left, as well as more coils of steel cable. Someone was hoisting large amounts of heavy rock here.

Right at the spot where two cable coils sit, the "heavy dotted line" path joins in from the right. We'll take that a little later. For now, follow the road uphill to where we see a fenced area come up on the right. Remains of the hoist platform are evident and there is another concrete platform across the path from it.

Peer through the fence for the most impressive sight yet, the deep dig of a major mine shaft. A large steel pipe sticks straight up through the dig, capped with a huge concrete block. There is also the opportunity for some archeological garbage exploration, as this must have been the town dumping area at some point. Old appliances rust in the trenches surrounding the mine. It is true that this hike is not exactly a "back to nature" experience. Let's hike up to the end of the road and then turn around and head back towards the orange trail. Once at the orange trail, do not continue to the left (east) but backtrack west a bit. Some stone foundations are on the north side of the trail and worth a peek. Now we can head east, passing point #8, and the Richard 2 shaft. This was the site of the mine's primary shaft, where ore was hoisted out by bucket. In 1884, a cart system was installed to replace the buckets. By 1886, close to 72,000 tons of iron ore were extracted. The mine was abandoned in 1903.

Interior of old building

Foundation wall

More vaguely recognizable ruins dot the area as we head toward post #9, site of the Mount Hope Mineral Railroad right-of-way. We've noticed the large number of railroad ties on this part of the trail. At the point where the orange trail veers to the left, a road appears straight before us and seems to be the logical extension of the trail. We'll leave the trail and go straight on the old rail bed for a little while. An impressive building ruin lies at the end, badly damaged and covered in graffiti. In fact, there is a great deal to see around here: railroad ties, foundations, remains of platforms and supports, and probably more hidden in the undergrowth.

Explore carefully and then look on the hillside above for the two water tanks perched there. A road leads up towards them. We'll take it and our friend the orange trail reveals itself quite soon. Back on orange, climbing up the hillside under the power lines, we can get to the tanks easily via a spur trail that is impossible to miss. At this point, we actually have some decent views to the south towards Mount Hope.

Continuing on the orange, we come to site #10: Turner's Whim Shaft, Trenton Iron Company's Shaft, Old Shafts 1 and 2, Whim Shaft 1, and Old Shaft 1. The earliest mine workings in the park occurred at this site, probably around 1830. The Richard vein was worked via the shallow pits seen here. Continue on to the junction of the red and orange trails, which we passed earlier. For the sake of completeness, we'll bear left (north) on red and follow it (passing the orange trail we followed earlier) straight back to the parking lot, making this trail a lazy figure eight through the old mine workings.

16

Open Adits

WHERE Harriman State Park, New York

WHY Two impressive iron mines that we can enter, plus historic shelter. Two Revolutionary War commemorative hiking trails add some historical interest.

DIFFICULTY Moderate, about 7.5 miles, significant elevation changes, with some bushwhacking and indistinct trails

MAP New York–New Jersey Trail Conference map 4, Harriman/Bear Mountain Trails (North)

UTM COORDINATES

Cranberry Mine	18 T 0579492, 4572749
Cranberry Mine, road near stream	18 T 0579402, 4572681
Cranberry Mine, air shaft	18 T 0579372, 4572635
Cranberry Mine, powder shed	18 T 0579359, 4572777
Cranberry Mine, building foundation	18 T 0579391, 4572702
Spanish Mine, opening on cliff face	18 T 0580332, 4570691
Spanish Mine, pit 1	18 T 0580410, 4570733
Spanish Mine, pit 2	18 T 0580448, 4570681

DIRECTIONS Palisades Interstate Parkway all the way north to the first traffic circle after the visitors' center. Take the circle around to Seven Lakes Drive South, and go 1.5 miles to the Silvermine Picnic Area.

¹ad-it *n.*: a horizontal opening or tunnel into a mine.

This one is an adventure, not for the timid. We'll need nerves of Parrott Brothers iron and our Big Flashlight.

We start from the Silvermine Ski Area parking lot on Seven Lakes Drive in Harriman State Park. Walk east on Seven Lakes Drive for 0.7 miles to where a stream passes under the roadway, just past the old stone bathrooms. As an aside, we'll run the hike in this direction because the trails heading up to the Cranberry Mine are hard to find going in the opposite direction.

Follow the stream uphill, heading north, for 0.4 miles on a gradual uphill slope. Be aware, because to find the first mine site we need to locate the old powder storage shed (18 T 0579359, 4572777) on the west side of the stream. It isn't hard to spot the shed with its leaning rusted metal door and stone walls covered by a curved, corrugated metal roof. It is partially sunken into the hillside and not a place that's inviting to enter. Black blasting powder and dynamite were stored here, first during mining operations and then in later years by the park.

After photographing the shed, we'll turn our back to the metal door and point to about two o'clock on the horizon (roughly 130° SE). If we look carefully we'll see a faint path outlined in that direction. Follow that bearing downhill for 0.1 mile, passing the rectangular stone-outlined foundation of a storage building (18 T 0579391, 4572702) as we approach the Cranberry Mine (18 T 0579402, 4572681). The mine entrance is facing northward, buried in a hillside.

Discovering the mine, it's hard not to be impressed. The opening is about 12 feet high, 20 or so feet wide, and has a stone pillar to the left, supporting the roof. During the 1920s, the adit was sealed off with

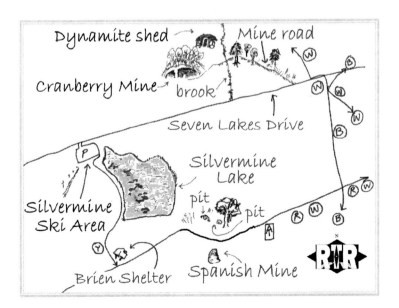

Powder shed

a cut stone wall but the center door has since been knocked down, thereby affording us entry. Don't even think about going in alone. Two flashlights per person are essential in case one of yours fails while we're exploring the mine.

The temperature difference inside is astounding. I measured a steady 65 degrees on a hot summer day after only a few steps inside. The tunnel heads off into the cold and humid darkness for a few hundred or so feet. Another tunnel we will soon encounter branches off to the right but doesn't go very far. The main shaft continues, bearing uphill and then ends, coincidentally, just as our nerve starts to. Drill holes are visible at the end of the shaft, toward the ceiling. This is an exciting mine to explore.

Iron was mined here around the turn of the century. After the mine was abandoned, the park used it to store dynamite until the 1930s.

After we're done with the mine, thanks to *Iron Mine Trails* we'll find there is a partially dug air shaft on top of the hill and due west of the entrance (18 T 0579372, 4572635). There are other exploration pits in the area, none especially remarkable, but check them out if you're in the mood. Follow the rocky ridge above the mine and you'll find them.

Let's make our way back to the stream. Locate the mine road that crosses it and then runs eastward from the mine. It's tricky to identify; look for the depression in the ground where the road is found (18 T 0579492, 4572749). Trust the trail map.

It quickly becomes apparent that few hikers use this old road. Deadfalls lie all over, making the path a challenge to pick out. Stay with it for 0.5 miles. Crossing a telephone pole line, the mine road suddenly ends without notice at another sizeable deadfall. Seven Lakes Drive is visible to the right, below us (we've heard the traffic for a while). We want to drop down quickly to the grassy plain below, but how the heck do we do it? And just where is the Anthony Wayne Trail, noted on our

Cranberry Mine looking out

Inside Cranberry Mine

map? The gravel pit in front of us postdates the mine road, obliterating it at a crucial junction. We must take the direct approach and cross over the fallen trees to the right to find the footpath down to the grassy area below. Once down, we can bushwhack the few yards over to Seven Lakes Drive and bear left (northeast), finally finding the white-square-blazed Anthony Wayne Trail where it appears after the old restroom building.

The AW, named for the great, portly Revolutionary War general "Mad" Anthony Wayne, follows Seven Lakes Drive for a short time before turning left (east) into the woods. We're only following it for a few yards but General Wayne has a remarkable story to tell.

Wayne came from a wealthy Pennsylvania family and had quite romantic notions about being in the military. His midnight attack upon the fort at Stony Point on July 16, 1779, is legend. After distinguishing himself in the Revolutionary War, he continued his military service fighting Indians in Ohio. Following his death in 1796, Wayne was buried at his request in Erie, Pennsylvania.

Thirteen years later, his son, Isaac, decided that his father's remains should be brought back to the family burial ground in Radnor, Pennsylvania. Isaac and his doctor traveled to Erie to exhume the body. Imagine their surprise to find the general nearly intact, with only a slight bit of rot on one foot. Bringing back the entire cadaver was impractical for them, since they had made their journey in a small wagon. The body was dissected by the doctor and the skeleton boiled for cleaning purposes. Mad Anthony's flesh and the flaying utensils stayed at the grave in Erie, while the cleansed skeleton went back to Pennsylvania for interment. Thus, the war hero has two burial places. It's been an honor hiking his trail.

The 1779 Trail (marked by round white discs with "1779" printed inside a diamond), commemorating the path of Wayne's victorious march upon the British-held fort at Stony Point in that year, will intersect the AW after a short time. In fact, we'll probably be hiking on it before we realize there has been a change of route. The map shows it as blue-blazed, but the actual discs marking the trail have a blue "1779" on a white background, making the trail intersection unclear. Staying to the right (south), we'll take the '79 for a pleasantly gradual ascent through blueberry bushes and ferns for 1.45 miles to the intersection of the 1779 and Appalachian Trail (white rectangles)/Ramapo-Dunderburg Trail (red dots on white).

Turn right (west). The AT/R-D starts off level but soon climbs up in a half mile or so to the 1,400-foot summit of Black Mountain, where the mysterious Spanish Mine sites await. Along the way, we're treated to our first high viewpoints to the south. Manhattan lies off in the distance, as do the Hudson River and the town of Haverstraw. To the north, through the trees, we can briefly glimpse Perkins Tower on top of Bear Mountain.

As we break for lunch, we have the opportunity to study the map and *Iron Mine Trails* for clues to the Spanish Mine sites. Legends abound regarding the origins of the mine. Did Captain Kidd really bury some of his treasure there (and also on Gardiner's Island, New York)? Did Spanish miners looking for silver in 1735 open the shafts? Will we be able to find the three sites associated with the Spanish Mine?

Spanish Mine

Let's start our exploration at the summit of Black Mountain, near a cairn. From that point, follow a bare rock path first to the north and then through grass to the east (about 140 feet from the cairn) to the first mine pit (18 T 0580410, 4570733). As usual, a tailings pile (waste rock removed from the mine) will give it away.

Retrace back to the cairn and go west on the trail. We'll see a post with an AT blaze soon; 60 feet down the trail from that point is a large rock, also AT-blazed. North of that rock, about 20 feet in and next to a stand of trees is the second mine pit (18 T 0580448, 4570681), deeper than the first and watered. Don't get too close because the ground is soft around the edge.

Well, all these holes in the ground are truly fascinating but we know from our research that the real goods are at the Spanish Mine adit about 100 feet down, dug into the south face of the cliff. There is no easy way to get to it. Follow the AT a short distance west, to a point at which it drops down sharply through a crevasse. At the bottom of that drop, leave the trail where it levels off and bushwhack around the cliff face eastward to a point where you are 100 feet or so below the rock cairn at the summit. Look for the mass of broken rock tailings for a clue as to where the mine is. The Spanish Mine adit (18 T 0580332, 4570691) is but a shallow dig into the rock but exciting nonetheless. The labor involved, from finding the site, to digging it out, to removing the ore, is mind-boggling. We can go a few feet in and survey the surrounding forest from within.

For our return to the trail, I found it easier to bushwhack straight up the cliff to the Appalachian Trail, rather than retrace our steps back around. We shouldn't be tempted to do that on the way down because we'd never find the mine and it is potentially dangerous climbing down without knowing exactly where we're heading (even with GPS codes).

Warning: The rock is loose in spots and the handholds can be uncertain. However we decide to do it, let's get back to the AT and continue west for 1.3 miles on our way to the Brien Memorial shelter.

The Civilian Conservation Corps built this shelter in 1933. According to *Harriman Trails*, William Brien was president of the New York Ramblers hiking club in 1923 and bequeathed funds for a shelter. The first shelter named for him was built at Island Pond in 1957 but was demolished in 1973 due to vandalism. This one, the former Letterrock Shelter, was renamed in his honor. The shelter is large, with two sets of bunk beds inside and a fire pit in front. We'll break here for a bit before the short trail back to Silvermine. Many AT through-hikers use this shelter before resuming their hike to Maine.

Because it is relatively close to the Silvermine parking area, this shelter sees a lot of day-trippers who make the short hike up here. There are guys and their girlfriends without backpacks, families with young children, spry grandmas and grandpas with the grandkids. As we pick up the yellow Menomine Trail back to the car, we'll more than likely see lots of folks hiking up here, no trail map in sight, completely unaware of the hidden treats tucked just off the track in this area.

17
Overlook Mountain House

WHERE ▪ On top of Overlook Mountain near Woodstock, New York

WHY ▪ Massive concrete ruins of a hotel, high viewpoint, fire tower

DIFFICULTY ▪ Moderate, about 5 miles round-trip, all uphill to the ruin

MAP ▪ New York–New Jersey Trail Conference map 41, Northern Catskill Trails

DIRECTIONS ▪ New York State Thruway (I-87) North to exit 19. Go west towards Pinehill on Route 28 for about 7 miles to Route 375. Make a right turn on 375 (north) towards Woodstock. Follow 375 to where it ends at Route 212, and turn left. From Route 212, head into the town center of Woodstock and make a right turn (north) on Ulster Co. 33. (The junction may not be signed. Look for a public parking sign at the turn.) Ulster Co. 33 will eventually turn right about a mile after the Route 212 intersection, but stay straight and follow the road (now Meads Mountain Road) to the signed Overlook parking area on your right.

There are few remains of the once magnificent cluster of huge mountain retreats that graced the Catskill Mountains region in the early 1900s. This hike will bring us to the best-preserved example of this group.

From the parking lot, follow the Overlook Spur Trail (red-blazed) 2.5 miles to the top. You can't get lost on this trail. It's pretty straightforward and climbs up to the summit on the old carriage road that served the hotel.

Well, not really *this* hotel exactly. The original Overlook House was built in 1871 and destroyed by fire in 1875. The second hotel, Catskill

Mountain House, was built on the site in 1878 and it also fell to fire in 1924. That structure was three stories high and anchored to the mountain via steel cables. Finally, someone had the idea to build a third hotel there out of fireproof poured concrete. The stock market crash of 1929 stopped work sometime around 1933 and what remains on top of the mountain is the never-completed concrete shell of this final venture, Overlook Mountain House and some other buildings.

Other massive Catskill Mountain hotels followed soon after the first such venture was successful, peaking in 1881 with the thousand-room-plus Hotel Kaaterskill at North Lake. Sadly, all have vanished, mainly due to fires. A circular day hike around the North/South Lake State Park area will bring you to the sites of two of these hotels, although nothing but a clearing remains of either of them (and therefore, that particular hike is not mentioned in this book).

The Overlook Spur Trail tops out by the hotel ruin at about 3,100 feet. Most of the hotel is easily accessible to our nosing around but some deep drops and overgrowth prohibit entry into other areas. Odd artifacts abound, including toilets, bathtubs, window frames, and fixtures. There are nonstop photo opportunities here. In addition to the main building, there is a smaller hotel structure behind the big ruin.

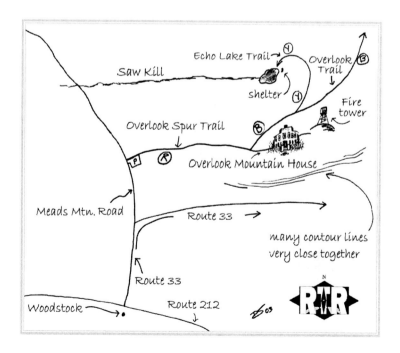

Overlook Hotel

After poking around, head over to the recently restored fire tower (sitting at 3,140 feet). This 60-foot structure has been here since 1950 and is one of five remaining original Catskill fire towers. Interestingly, parts of it are from an older 1927 tower that stood on Gallis Hill, near Kingston. After a nerve-testing climb up the tower to the 7-foot-square cabin on top, we can see the Berkshire Hills in Massachusetts over to the east, the regal Hudson River in front of them, and the Taconic

Another view of Overlook Hotel

Side view of Overlook Hotel

Mountains in New York. The Ashokan Reservoir and the Shawangunk Mountains are on our side of the river to the south. Our lunch spot is at the picnic table down below.

Walking to the east of the fire tower brings us to a high ledge with about 2,000 feet of air below us. Carved into this ledge are names and dates from over a hundred years ago, if you believe all of them. Let's face it, anyone can carve "David 1802" into stone and make it seem authentic. There's no way to tell what is real and what is a hoax, although I do believe most of them are actually historic graffiti. Some of the carvings took some time to do and are impressively skillful.

We'll take our time enjoying the view and the ruins, then it's back down the Overlook Spur Trail to our car. Maybe we'll do some dinner and faux-hippie gawking in Woodstock before we drive home.

18

The Pergola

WHERE · Palisades Interstate Park, New Jersey, beginning at the State Line Lookout

WHY · Abandoned sections of old Route 9W, Peanut Leap (or Half Moon) Falls, remains of the fanciful Italian Garden, Giant Stairs, Women's Federation monument, Burnett-Timken estate remains

DIFFICULTY · Moderate, about 6 miles round-trip, with some steep ascents and descents

MAP · New York–New Jersey Trail Conference map 4A, Hudson Palisades Trails, New Jersey section

WEB SITE · www.njpalisades.org

DIRECTIONS · Palisades Interstate Parkway northbound to the State Line Lookout parking area near exit 3.

Relatively new discoveries await us as we begin our explorations of the Hudson Palisades. We usually pass the Palisades on our way up to other parks, such as Harriman. I've always known that there were interesting ruins and historic sites in this region but it wasn't until I started researching this book that I discovered exactly what the story is here. In this chapter, we will encounter ruins of sculpted gardens, an old mansion site, a state line boundary marker obelisk, a castle-like monument, and an abandoned roadbed.

There are actually a few old mansion sites and worthy ruins in Palisades Interstate Park. The problem is that much of the Long Path, which passes by the best ruins, also runs along the Palisades Interstate

Parkway. For me, this negates the nature experience because the traffic noise is intrusive. If you're interested, the section of the LP above and below the park headquarters has plenty of fun remains to seek out. The park sponsors historic hikes during the summer to many of these sites. For details see www.njpalisades.org/calendar.htm and look for the "Millionaires Row" tour.

The Lookout Inn at the State Line Lookout area is a fine (seasonal) spot to buy a lunch "to go" for our journey, or to peruse assorted books of historic interest. Once inside, be sure to look for various displayed pamphlets and brochures that outline the many ski trails and unmarked paths that lace the area. As in much of Palisades Interstate Park (which includes Harriman and Bear Mountain State Parks), the Works Progress Administration was responsible for constructing the inn and many of the more impressive trail "aids" (steps, etc.) that we will encounter and, as usual, they did a thoroughly professional job.

After we get our gear together, let's walk over to the scenic over-look and check out the view. Hawks circle lazily about, taking advantage of the swirling updrafts caused by the cliffs. It's a sheer 500-foot drop down to the Hudson River, as it is in many other spots along our trail. Due caution is strongly advised. The only higher cliffs I know of are on Breakneck Ridge. Hastings-on-Hudson is directly across the river on the New York side. Yonkers is further south; Dobbs Ferry is to the north.

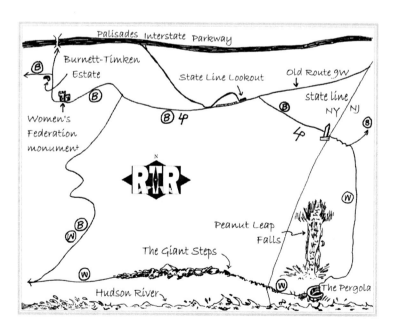

We begin by walking over to the northern end of the lot, near the inn, and locating the blue-blazed Long Path (which runs along the unused 1926 Route 9W for a short time). Let's take it, eventually separating from old 9W as we head into the woods. There is a wooden sign at the split, indicating various trail destinations. After about a half hour of walking, a concrete New York–New Jersey state boundary marker looms ahead on the left side of the trail, placed when a modern survey laid out the definitive border, which had been in dispute since colonial times. The fence behind it marks the property line between Palisades Interstate Park and the Lamont-Doherty Earth Observatory. The trail runs through their property for a short time. Continue on the LP as it follows the fence for a short time and then passes through a gate into New York State. The trail runs northerly across sheer cliff tops with a steel-cabled fence preventing unfortunate 500-foot mistakes.

The Tappan Zee Bridge in New York State is now visible ahead of us, running from Tarrytown on the east shore to Nyack on the west. The bridge name comes from the Tappan Indian tribe of the area, and "zee," Dutch for "sea." When I was in Holland some years ago, I asked a tour guide for some translations of New York place names. He told me that Tappan Zee translates roughly to "pouring sea," as "tappan" means "pour" in Dutch. Think of a beer tap. But officially, it's the Native American reference that gets the credit. Below the Tap on the left (west side) is the town of Piermont, with its famous artificial land pier running a mile into the Hudson, and below that sits the largest saltwater marsh on the river.

Most of the hiking consists of rock hopping as we quickly descend towards the river. After about an hour of hiking (and about fifteen or so minutes of walking past the gate), the LP drops steeply downhill on endless WPA steps. The river seems to be getting closer up to now but at this point the trail veers sharply to the left (west), crosses two wooden foot bridges and then meets up with the northern terminus of the white-blazed Shore Trail. The following wooden sign is posted at the intersection:

Shore Trail
Warning: Hiking Very Difficult Next Two Miles

Is that amusing or ominous? Either way, the white Shore Trail descends eastward rapidly, bordering a cascade on the right and streams coming in from the left (in wet weather). Wooden boards secured tightly across the path aid the hapless hiker on the steepest sections. The trail can get muddy and slippery. I know—I slipped on the slick mud and tumbled downhill a few yards, scratched up the

Pergola

length of my right arm, and smacked my leg against a rock, bruising it from hip to knee. I hobbled painfully down the trail past the Peanut Leap waterfall (sometimes known as Half Moon Falls, in honor of Henry Hudson's ship) to the safe haven of the offbeat Italian Garden ruin at the base of the falls.

Mary Lawrence Tonnetti has forever cemented her name in park lore as the creator of the Italian Garden. At the turn of the century, she was a well-known artist (and 1900s-era hippie) from a wealthy family. Traveling in Italy, she became enamored with the architecture and, once she returned home, transformed a family-owned property at the base of the falls into her own eccentric party spot. She built platforms, staircases, heavy stone walls, arched alcoves, and reflecting pools with lion's-head fountains on the site. She entertained her New York art crowd friends with exotic parties, spaghetti dinners, and various other artistic events there. Most famous was "The Pergola," a small colonnaded sitting area right on the shore of the Hudson River. Above the columns was a semicircular concrete rail draped with grape vines. All in all, the garden was a fanciful spot that was a favorite of travelers, and still is.

As is the case so often, time, the elements, and vandals have leveled the place to the reduced condition it is in now. The steps are broken. The Pergola columns are in pieces along the ground, visible only if you go looking for them. The reflecting pools are filled in with

Pergola steps

debris and barely recognizable. The falls remain strong, though, and
you can still sit quietly on the Pergola benches and reflect on the river.
With some imagination, we can still fabricate what must have been
here, and possibly even hear the echoes of those long-gone avante
garde parties. We will undoubtedly have company as we rest here, as
other hikers come by to investigate the garden. This is one of the most
popular hiking destinations in the park and I'm certain Mary would
like that.

Dave on the Italian Garden steps

The white Shore Trail heads southward, following the mighty Hudson River as it brings us through the Giant Steps section of the route. The steps aren't especially giant but there are many of them, sometimes comically so. It's slow going crossing the Giant Steps because it's all high-impact pounding on your ankles and knees for 2 miles.

Finally, the blue/white trail appears and we begin the arduous ascent to the top of the cliffs. Slow and steady is the way to do it; never sit down and rest only briefly as you trudge up the 500 feet from river to Long Path.

Once we meet the Long Path, bear left (south) and take it 0.2 miles to the Women's Federation Watchtower, a monument to the organization that began founding the Palisades Interstate Park in the early part of the twentieth century to protect the cliffs from the increasing amount of blasting that was going on at the time. The rock that was being removed from the cliffs was used for Manhattan skyscrapers and ship's ballast. We can climb up the short staircase to the top level and take in the river view that the Federation worked so hard to preserve. Just down the trail (to the south) is the site of the Burnett-Timken estate, one of the many "mansion" sites that the Long Path features as it makes its way through the palisades.

Artist Cora Timken and scientist John Burnett did experiments with magnetism in their copper-domed lab on this site. The only identifiable remains are of the pool just off the LP, a few yards south of the Women's Federation monument, near an intersection with a dirt road. The lab was destroyed by fire in 1939 and if that wasn't bad enough, Cora's artwork was stored inside. Someplace out of sight is their bomb shelter. It's underneath us somewhere, 100 feet long and hand-carved out of the rock.

The construction plans for the Palisades Interstate Parkway called for the road to go right through the Burnett property. A year after Cora's death, the family was awarded $1.5 million for the plot. The state razed parts of the estate but never did completely demolish it. We'll return to our vehicles by traveling northward on the blue-blazed Long Path, enjoying one of the few sections of the trail that is removed from the ever-present parkway.

19

Ramapo Valley County Reservation

WHERE Near Mahwah, New Jersey

WHY Mill ruin, high views, two old mines, an estate foundation, two house ruins, active scout camp out of season

DIFFICULTY Challenging, 9 miles with significant elevation changes

MAPS New York–New Jersey Trail Conference map 22, North Jersey Trails

UTM COORDINATES
Nickel Mine 1   18 T 0566932, 4549332
Nickel Mine 2   18 T 0566919, 4549354

DIRECTIONS New York State Thruway (I-87) North to exit 15, Route 287 South/Route 17 South. Once on the ramp, bear left immediately and exit onto Route 17 South. Continue to Route 202 (Ramapo Valley Road) and bear left at the end of the exit ramp towards Ramapo College. Begin at the Ramapo State Forest parking area, about 2 miles west of Route 17 in Mahwah, New Jersey.

Many smaller attractions add up to an outstanding day in the woods on this hike in northern New Jersey. For best results, do this particular hike in the fall or winter, when the scout camp will most likely be empty. Be advised that the trail map distributed by the park is inaccurate and should not be trusted. Our route will bring us up to the Nickel Mine and, crossing into Ringwood State Park, the Butler Mine and some viewpoints. The Boy Scout camp and some ruins round out the day.

As with most ore-bearing regions, this one, too, had mines, sawmills, and foundries. It was also logged to the ground, probably more than once. The Hopkins and Dickinson Manufacturing Company in Darlington processed much of the ore that was mined here. A. B. Darling, of Darlington fame, eventually bought the property and turned it into his estate. We'll visit what's left of his house when we're done hiking.

Right away, we notice the mill ruin on the river. We'll pick up the first trail by crossing the bridge into the park and continuing straight on the silver trail past Scarlet Oak Pond. The blue-blazed Ridge Trail comes in shortly. Let us begin our ascent up to the Nickel Mine. The hiking trails in this part of the park are mostly on woods roads.

At 1.1 miles past the parking lot, the Havemeyer Trail (blue/white-blazed) terminates at the Ridge Trail. Distances in this park are deceiv-

Nickel Mine
site

ing. It doesn't seem that long on the map but it's taken almost an hour just to get to this point. Once we're at the junction of the Havemeyer and Ridge Trails, face south, looking back the way we came along the Ridge Trail. The Havemeyer Trail is now on our left.

Point to the two o'clock position on the horizon with your right hand. Heading a few hundred feet down the embankment on that bearing (southwesterly) will bring us to the Nickel Mine. There are two mine pits on a level shelf at the site. One is circular and flooded and surrounded by tailings (18 T 0566932, 4549332). A few feet to the east is a flooded trench with drainage at the west end (18 T 0566919, 4549354).

The Hopkins and Dickinson Manufacturing Company did some exploratory work in these mountains. They were looking for iron and nickel but mines such as this never produced ore on any meaningful scale.

Retrace back to the blue Ridge Trail and we'll continue to the next mine, the Butler. Follow the blue around to the silver trail, where we bear to the right (northwesterly) and continue to the red/silver trail, taking that to the right and up. There is a new orange-blazed trail appearing that is not on any map that I have, so we'll just ignore it. At some point around here, we left Ramapo Valley County Reservation and entered into Ringwood State Park.

After an invigorating climb, we finally reach Bear Swamp Lake. (After almost two hours of walking, you'd think we'd have covered more ground.) Here, blazes get a bit funny. The blue-blazed Shore Trail circles the lake and conjoins with the Cannonball Trail (blazed by a red C).

The historic Cannonball Trail supposedly follows old roads to un-named mining and foundry sites where ordinance was manufactured in Revolutionary days. As far as I can tell this is all legend. The real problem here is that the Cannonball is possibly the worst-marked regional trail that I've come across. It makes its way along but the blazes in this area are of little help if indeed this is the trail you're try-ing to follow. It deteriorates even more over to the west in Ramapo Mountain State Forest, where we'll be looking for a mansion ruin on another day. Anyway, bear to the right (north) and try to follow the dual Cannonball/Shore Trail (blue-blazed) as it hugs the lake. This is a good spot for a short rest.

Afterward, continue around the lake on the blue Shore Trail. (What do you know, the Cannonball has been following us all along.

Noah explores the old mill

Noah at the
Nickel Mine

Wouldn't know it by the blazes.) The yellow Hoeferlin Trail joins up on the opposite side of the lake. By the way, the New York–New Jersey Trail Conference map is correct in blaze designation here, so don't follow the county map. Yellow and blue blazes run concurrently for a few yards, bearing southwest, until the blue bears left and the yellow heads to the right. Take yellow and climb up to the Butler Mine.

It isn't hard to find the Butler. It runs alongside the trail 0.2 miles northeast of the Crossover Trail (white-blazed). The Butler was the site of exploration digs and activity from the middle of the 1860s through the 1880s. There are a series of pits and trenches on the site, easily found by the trail. We've worked hard to get here so it's now officially lunch time. Elevation at this point is about 1,100 feet. After lunch, it's back on yellow and headed in the same direction (south).

Enough with the mines right now, let's find some views. Continuing on yellow, passing the white Crossover Trail ultimately brings us to Ilgenstein Rock, a fine lookout at about 1,100 feet. Bear Swamp Lake is below us and on a clear day we can see Manhattan. Continue on yellow and soon we'll get to Erskine Lookout, this time looking out to the west and Wanaque Reservoir. Pick up the green-blazed trail that meets the yellow-blazed trail at Erskine Lookout. Again, at this point the Trail Conference map is correct and the county map is not.

The green trail drops and unexpectedly reaches Camp Yaw Paw on Cannonball Lake, still in use as a Boy Scout camp. In the off-season it appears to be abandoned at first glance but soon we see clearly that it is not. There are lots of buildings and lean-tos around the property to explore, most of them locked and secured.

Gathering back in camp, we have a decision to make. If time and daylight allow, we can find the yellow-blazed Hoeferlin Trail (according to the map, the Cannonball is also somewhere around here) and follow it westward down to the yellow/silver trail, then eastward (left) past a ruin and back to the car. On my last visit, the trails were very poorly marked in this section and I found it simpler to just follow the camp road down to the ruin. The other advantage to this route is that we parallel a series of cascades as we descend. A major disadvantage is that walking downhill on asphalt is hard on hiking-boot-clad feet. However you get there, the twin buildings of the ruin are just off the camp road at the junction of the yellow/silver trail. What the heck were they? Inquiries at this point have proven fruitless so your guess is as good as mine.

The yellow/silver trail to the left (east) goes up and over Matty Price Hill as it heads back to the silver trail and our car. We feel this one. Although the mileage on this hike was only about 9, our feet are saying it was more!

Postscript: Although we're done hiking, before we drive home let's turn right and head down Route 202 for about 0.3 miles and see the curved driveway and huge stone foundation of Mr. Darling's estate, where there are some good exploring opportunities. There's a better view of it if you go further downhill past the driveway and then turn around.

20

The Roomy Mine

WHERE ≡ Norvin Green State Forest, New Jersey

WHY ≡ A big iron mine that we can enter, panoramic high viewpoint along the way

DIFFICULTY ≡ Challenging, 10 miles with significant elevation changes and possible water-crossing issues

MAP ≡ New York–New Jersey Trail Conference map 21, North Jersey Trails

UTM COORDINATES
Blue Mine   18 T 0557366, 4545594
Roomy Mine   18 T 0557512, 4546142

DIRECTIONS ≡ Route 80 West to exit 53, Route 23 North. Continue about 10 miles to Route 511 and make a right turn towards the town of Butler. Follow 511 as it snakes through Butler. Make a left at Hamburg Turnpike (first left after Arch Street). Bear right on Glenwild Road as it goes uphill and look for the yellow blazes at a pullout on the right after a mile or so. Glenwild Road is also called Otter Hole Road.

This investigation is unusual in that there's plenty of hiking but only two sites for us to discover, one being a flooded mine and the other being the real goods: a large enterable magnetite iron mine with an impressive adit, so be sure to bring the Big Flashlight along. We'll do plenty of walking on the way there and back. Climbing to high points and negotiating some challenging water crossings keep things from getting dull. Many trials lie ahead in our path.

Starting out on the yellow-blazed trail, we'll follow as it winds through a low swampy area, frequently hopping rocks to cross over the streams. In summer, there is usually no trouble crossing but spring snow melt or rain in other months can make things complicated. Unless you plan on getting soaked, do another hike in this book in wet weather and come back here when things dry out.

Yellow climbs to an intersection with the Hewitt Butler Trail (blue-blazed), totally appropriate nomenclature for an iron mine investigation because Abraham Hewitt was an ironmaster in Ringwood during the busy years (and maybe Butler refers to the nearby town?). The Highland Trail, which will someday be a long-distance route, joins up and keeps us company for the first half of this route. Yellow veers off shortly, but blue is what we want. The trail turns sharply to the left (north) at a point where a white trail begins.

Climbing up Carris Hill, starting at about 550 feet and topping out at 1,000, is a long process with a steady ascent. We must remember to look around when we reach the rocky sides for the first viewpoints of

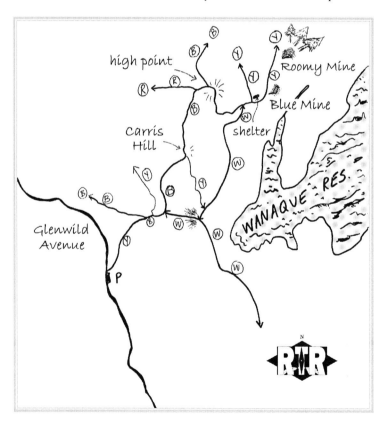

Trail
to high point

the trip. When we reach the intersection with the yellow Carris Trail, we know we've hit the summit. At about 1,000 feet, this point is actually 100 feet higher than the "high point" we're heading to, but the views aren't as impressive. Continuing northward, we pass more views and travel through coniferous forest while we go up and down, seemingly forever.

Approaching the high point where the blue and red trails come together, the real climb begins with a short scramble up slick bald rocks and past scrubby pines. Hot summer days will find us in the middle of a crowd as we scout out a suitable lunch spot. The Wanaque Reservoir (pronounced "wanakie") is about 800 feet below us and the spires of Manhattan are in the distance to the east. We'll rest here for a little while and enjoy the view before the push to the mines.

After our break, we'll pick up the red Wyanokie Crest Trail on a steep downhill track to more water crossings. Take note of the white trail we pass on the right—that's the way back. Soon enough a yellow trail joins up. Because you've done your research and looked at the Trail Conference map before starting out, you know the mines are along the yellow Mine Trail, but beware! The Mine Trail is a loop and we want to continue straight, so don't make the left.

High Point Rock

Walking along yellow will bring us past a run-down, uninviting shelter. It's in poor repair at the bottom of the hill and so there isn't any view like the Harriman shelters have. I can't imagine why anyone would want to stay there. The only good thing about it is once we see it we know that the Blue Mine is coming up.

The Blue Mine (18 T 0557366, 4545594) sits on a shelf just above Blue Mine Brook, which is crossed by a sturdy wooden bridge.

Wyanokie high point approach

Although flooded, the mine is a worthy objective just because it's so big. It was active sometime in the 1850s, part of the Ringwood group of mines. Flooding was always a problem during the years it was in operation, with several shutdowns taking place while the water was removed. The mine was last worked around 1905. Just to the left of the opening, a concrete pad and block supported the dewatering pump.

About a half mile down yellow sits the star of our show, the Roomy Mine (18 T 05575112, 4546142). It was opened around 1840, providing magnetite iron ore. On one of my visits, the leader of a Boy Scout troop was sticking magnets on the rocks, to the surprise of the scouts (and, I must confess, myself, also). One of you is looking unhappily at

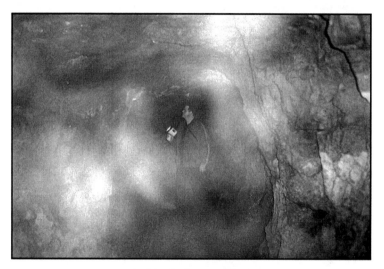

Inside the Roomy Mine

that small opening in front of us and thinking, "That's it? You can't be serious. Is there anything *impressive* about this mine that we're hiking our butts off to see?" All I can say is "Get your flashlight out."

First, shuck off your pack, toss it through the opening, and get ready to crawl. Don't leave it behind while we enter the mine. I bring my pack anytime I enter a mine, even if it's only for a short distance. Just in case something awful happens, I want my gear with me, such as a lighter, first aid, food, water, and a signal whistle, to name just a few items. I wouldn't be happy if I was stuck somewhere and my pack was just a few feet out of reach or behind a rock fall.

The low passage going into the mine is about 1.5 feet high. We need to get down in the dirt on our hands and knees to wiggle through. Once in, there is a large room on the other side that is open to the sky,

Leaving the Roomy Mine

with the adit proper just in front of us. It's about 6 feet high and wide enough for two people to walk side by side for a bit. The rounded tunnel snakes along for 50 or so feet. Bats reside inside and are easy to spot as they huddle inside drill holes and crevices. We can walk to the end and then do something *everyone* does, which is shut off the flashlights and experience absolute darkness.

This particular mine is unusual in that we can enter legally and safely. The only other mines I know of that look like this are on the Copper Mine Trail in the Delaware Water Gap. There are two mines in that group, but sometimes they are closed off and sealed to visitation (thus they aren't mentioned in this book).

The walk back begins when our mine exploration ends. This can easily turn into a six-hour hike so, without wasting too much time, let's head back to the white Lower Trail, taking it westward around the bases of Wyanokie Crest and Carris Hill. Of note along the way is the intersection with the yellow Carris Trail (we saw the top of the trail earlier today) and a T-bone intersection where the white Lower Trail ends. The trail it connects with is also white (the Post Brook Trail), which can be confusing. Bearing to the right (west) puts us onto the Post Brook Trail toward Chickahokie Falls. In times of high water, the challenges begin here.

If it's dry out, we have a 40-minute walk from the falls back to the vehicles. If it's after rain or a snow melt, it could take longer and I'm telling you there is *no way* to cross a fast-flowing Post Brook and stay dry because there are no easy rock or tree bridge crossings. When we got caught in this situation one cold December day, the RTR Investigation Team had to take off shoes and socks and cross the first wide, frigid stream we came to, reboot, and then tackle the crossing near the falls. That one got both of us soaked, but fortunately the cars weren't far.

The Post Brook Trail ends at the blue Hewitt Butler Trail we started on, and that in turn brings us back to the yellow trail. Turning left (south) brings us back to the car after a seriously long day of peak bagging, iron mine hunting, and stream jumping.

21
Southford Falls State Park

WHERE ▪ Southford, Connecticut

WHY ▪ Mill foundations, covered bridge, waterfalls and cascades, fire tower

DIFFICULTY ▪ Easy, about 2 miles round-trip with negligible rise

MAP ▪ Park trail map (available online)

WEB SITE ▪ http://dep.state.ct.us/stateparks/parks/southford.htm

DIRECTIONS ▪ From I-84 East, take exit 16, following Connecticut Route 188 South for about 3 miles into the town of Southford. Follow to junction with Route 67. At the traffic light, take a left onto Route 67. At the next light, take a right back onto Route 188. There is only one brown sign pointing to the park entrance on the left, so be alert.

The physical remains of a former match factory that was once on this site are minimal but this attractive, small, 120-acre state park makes for a pleasurable afternoon of exploration. This is a good park for young hikers because of the easy terrain and fire tower lookout.

Eightmile Brook was first used as a power source in the early 1800s, when a fulling mill (for manufacturing wool clothing), gristmill, and sawmill were erected. Eventually, ownership changed hands and in 1849 the fulling mill was used to manufacture paper. A new mill was built in 1855, using old rags to make paper. A button and a hardware factory joined the group soon afterward, with the brook supplying power to all of them.

By 1868, the site above the falls included three paper mills, a repair shop, gristmill, sawmill, cutlery shop, and an axe handle factory.

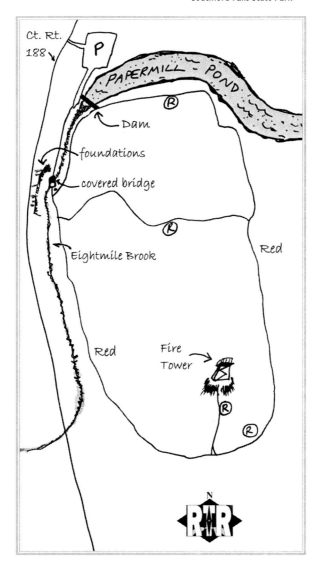

Below the falls stood a butcher shop, hotel, and blacksmith shop. In 1881, the paper mill burned in a fire but was rebuilt soon afterward.

The Diamond Match Company acquired the property in 1901, making paperboard for matches, though not their actual striking heads. Roughly a hundred Southford residents worked in the factory for a period of about twenty-one years. Employee housing and a baseball field stood in the spot where the parking lot is today. By 1922, production had ceased and a suspicious fire destroyed the dormant factory

Southford Falls State Park

buildings. In 1926, the State of Connecticut acquired the land for use as a park. But there was work to be done to make the area safe.

In the spring of 1934, the Civilian Conservation Corps dug out the burned ruins and debris and began the process of improving the new park for recreation. By 1948, land acquisitions were completed and the park area doubled.

We won't get too upset if we don't have the park trail map with us, since there is only one red-blazed trail circling the park, with a red-blazed spur trail at the halfway point that leads off to the fire tower. For our purposes, we will circle counterclockwise so we get to see the foundations first.

Heading towards the dam on Papermill Pond, we'll pass some picnic benches, a grindstone, and two information boards. A faded trail map is displayed on the second board, but it isn't very helpful. Resist the urge to cross the path across the pond . . . we'll do that later. Follow the path along the pond, past the curved dam overflow. More picnic benches lie past the spillway and there is an opportunity to trace Eightmile Brook as it spills over the dam and cascades down towards the covered bridge and beyond.

Stone foundations near the covered bridge give some indication to the size of the mills that once were here. Burr Arch Bridge (built in 1972) is the second such covered bridge on this site. Passing through, it takes us from the town of Southbury to Oxford. Once we cross the bridge, some investigating will reveal minor foundations to the left and a water conduit in the brook. Keep on the red-blazed trail, following it southward. The brook parallels along on our right, sometimes in a deep ravine. The trail is wide and easy to follow, occasionally crossing muddy sections or streams on a boardwalk.

Eightmile Brook, and Route 188 beyond, eventually veer off to the west while the trail bears easterly through evergreens on the way to the tower spur. Going on our counterclockwise circuit, we will more easily spot the sign pointing towards the tower spur trail (it can be easy to miss when walking in the other direction). Once we find our spur, let's follow it for 0.1 miles to the small fire tower perched upon a hill. It is a sturdy wood and metal affair, not nearly as rickety as other fire towers we have come across in our adventures. There is a fine 360-degree view of the surrounding hills from up here, and it could be a worthy lunch destination.

Once we're done here, we will continue in the same counter-clockwise direction on the red trail, eventually coming back to the beginning. There is a seasonal snack bar and some outhouses at the pond that we will pass, and the water itself is a nice place to spend a little time at the end of the hike.

22

Watchung Reservation

WHERE Mountainside, New Jersey

WHY Deserted Village of Feltville, two abandoned quarries, Suicide Tower, two mill ruins, copper mine, Magic Forest, historic cemetery, Nike missile base site, horrific predators frozen in time

DIFFICULTY Moderate, about 8 miles with relatively minor elevation changes

MAP Watchung Reservation trail map and *Deserted Village of Feltville* pamphlet, available at the Nature and Science Center

CONTACT Trailside Nature and Science Center, 452 New Providence Road, Mountainside, NJ 07092; 908-789-3670

DIRECTIONS Take I-78 West to exit 43, New Providence/Berkeley Heights. After the exit ramp merges with Hill Road, make a right at the first traffic light onto McMane Avenue, and go straight to where it ends at Glenside Avenue (Route 527). Left on Glenside (note the closed-off road that passes over the highway and heads uphill because we'll mention it later in the hike), right on W. R. Tracy Drive (Route 645), and at the traffic circle turn right on Summit Lane. Follow the signs to the Trailside Nature and Science Center.

This is a weird one, folks, so let's get started.

The 2,000-acre Watchung Reservation has a sinister quality that is impossible to ignore. Murder, suicide, a self-styled emperor's autocratic rule, floating limbs, whispers of past satanic rituals, and the Cold War all play a part. We'll get into the details as we do our exploration, but to experience the effect to its fullest we must carefully plan the appropriate sort of day for this hike. Sunny summer days full of blooming flora, chirping birds, and playing children just won't do; instead we'll pick a gloomy day near the end of winter, when the newer pines are enshrouded by a low gray fog, a hint of rain is in the air, and the older deciduous trees gently wave their bare branches at us through the mist in mute warning of the real and imagined horrors that await us just down the trail.

Even the name Watchung has a vaguely ominous sound, a sort of comic-book sound effect of axe hitting bone. In reality, it comes from the Lenape word for "high hills," a reference to the topography north of the park.

The local deer population, whose numbers have grown too quickly for their own good, have reason for their own instinctive concern. As I drove to the trailhead, I spotted a few that met a sudden end via auto on the side of the road. To control the exploding numbers, the county has controversially authorized seasonal culls under police supervision. Signs are conspicuously posted when the culling is in session, warning careless hikers to stay on the trails, to resist bushwhacking. On the trail or not, gunfire is not something you ever want to hear while hiking.

For purposes of navigation, we have to recognize the difference between bridle trails (solid lines) and foot paths (dotted lines), as indicated on the park map. Be advised that this park has a reputation for

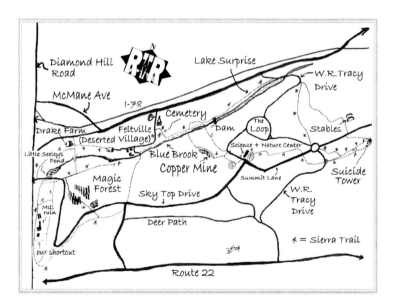

changing trail colors. It's also worth noting that many of the trails are often very muddy throughout the park, so waterproof footwear is essential for insuring comfort and dry socks.

Our adventure begins at the Nature and Science Center, next to the Planetarium. We'll start early in the morning so we can finish up during their operating hours (1–5 P.M.), thereby experiencing the unique terrors that dwell within those innocuous walls.

The white-square-blazed Sierra Trail is the main trail in this park, forming a 10.5-mile loop as it goes along, frequently conjoining with other blazed trails. Following the Sierra Trail from the Nature and Science Center in a northwesterly direction will soon lead us past our first site, an old copper mine dug out of a brook running through a deep ravine. The broken rock littering the area clearly reflects the patina of oxidized copper, though most of it is worthless basalt. It is believed that this mine was merely a test dig sometime in the 1700s, predating the other endeavors we'll soon uncover. The mud, sometimes ankle-deep, sucks relentlessly at our waterproof hiking boots as we pass through.

We're now heading downhill as a blue trail joins the Sierra. Soon we'll see the slow-moving, shallow Blue Brook ahead of us. The brook is an outflow of Lake Surprise, which was dammed at the western end in the mid-1800s to provide power for David Felt's paper mill.

We'll leave the Sierra for a bit and follow Blue Brook to the west. At the point where the next bridle trail connects at a bridge, if we cross over we can inspect the slim remains of David Felt's paper mill along the brook. We'll find out a little more about that enterprise a bit later in the afternoon when we explore the Deserted Village. Cross over the bridge again and follow the bridal path uphill, eventually passing a group of private homes on our left. The lights from these homes, shining coldly through the trees, have undoubtedly stirred the imaginations of young adults looking for a scare as they explore the park after hours because they're visible for quite a distance in subdued light.

Bearing directly south (left), we'll follow the bridle trail as it crosses Sky Top Drive and then heads in a southwesterly direction for 0.26 miles (from the road) to another junction with the Sierra Trail. Following the white squares, we cross the road once again and come to the Sky Top Picnic Area.

A major advantage to taking this hike out of season or during the week is that this usually busy place is hushed and empty. Noisy crowds would just destroy the mood we're working so hard to create! A covered area with some picnic tables, the inside roof strangely painted in a sort of camouflage, might shield us from the drizzle for a while as we

Magic Forest

consider the dense woods a few yards past the protection of the shelter. Let's take a short break here before journeying up the trail into the
enigmatic Magic Forest.

It's known to area residents as either the Enchanted Forest or the
Magic Forest but whatever it's called, this is one unusual place. Actually
a pine plantation courtesy of the Civilian Conservation Corps around
1930, the area features 16,000 pine trees planted in endless ruler-
straight rows, with all the trees inside being the exact same distance
apart from each other. When you hear whispers of furtive late-night
rituals or Satan worship in the Watchung Reservation, this is ground
zero. Downed trees and dead stumps seem to echo the suspicion that
robed figures are loitering in the shadows, just waiting for us to leave
so they can continue their evil rites. Park personnel and the Mountainside Police have told me there is no basis to these stories. The mysterious lights that are sometimes seen flickering down the paths after dark
are from the private homes nearby, just outside the reservation.

Although the white square blazes head straight down one of the
rows, it's absolutely impossible to stay on the trail. The pines are all the
same height and circumference and all have tall straight trunks that are
completely barren of low branches. You wander off, photographing the
weird patterns that the rows create, looking up at the sky (if we're
unfortunate enough to be here on a nice day) through the trees, won-
dering about all those fallen pines that break up the monotony of the
straight rows, and then you suddenly realize that you can't find the trail!
The ground is absolutely flat and all the rows look alike. Getting one's
bearings or finding a point of reference is nearly impossible. That old

uncomfortable feeling of not knowing where you are takes hold. It begins with unease and then quickly graduates to serious concern. Am I really lost? Where's the trail? Was someone looking at me through the trees?

Getting back on the trail successfully when you've lost the way is what separates the experts from the amateurs in the hike leader game, so naturally we're soon back on track, heading north through this strange artificial forest. At the next bridle trail junction, the Sierra turns to the right (east) but we're going to the left (west). At 0.2 miles, the trail crosses Sky Top Drive at a parking area next to Little Seeley's Pond, and there's the Sierra again on the other side of the road.

We aren't taking it. Instead, we'll pick up the footpath that follows Blue Brook, eventually passing a dam and a series of smaller cascades downstream. To no one's surprise, the Sierra again appears, goes up and over an escarpment, and then delivers us to an impressive home foundation with a brick pillar next to it, presumably from a gate. A mill foundation is just down the trail, as is a rock cut that fed water to the mill. The park naturalist told me this might be a natural formation due to the fact there are no tool or blast marks in the rock, but I disagree. We've walked through too many man-made cuts on these explorations not to recognize one when our feet are upon it.

There are plenty of interesting artifacts at this mill site to uncover as we rummage around. The only thing dampening our cautious enthusiasm is the traffic noise from New Providence Road on the other side of the brook. There is what appears to be a steam boiler buried along the path near the old mill. The hillside to our left is loaded with broken rock from an old quarry.

As we approach the end of the escarpment to our left an old road appears, presumably from the days when the mill was in operation. Turning left (southeasterly), we'll save a few steps by taking the old road up to a fire ring, where we'll then see the trail just above us. We again bear left (northerly) and follow the Sierra back to Sky Top Drive. That little shortcut saved us about fifteen minutes of walking and spared us the indignity of hiking past a noisy rock quarry operation and construction site.

For the next 2 or 3 miles we're sticking with the Sierra Trail, so after a short rest our hike continues. The trail bears left (west) at Sky Top Drive and then goes sharply to the right into the woods. After crossing a boardwalk, the Sierra makes a left on a foot trail and then turns right in short order, but we aren't going right just yet. Straight past the Sierra junction on the path, the 1940s-era Drake's Farm site appears on the left side of the trail, consisting of a brambly rock-lined foundation. Not much is known about the history of the site, so after we're done snooping around (looking for a spring somewhere in the vicinity) we'll continue through the gloom on white for 0.6 miles to the major historic site in this park, the Deserted Village of Feltville.

Some of my information about Feltville comes from the park's self-touring pamphlet. Feltville (known in later years as Glenside Park) has had many different incarnations since the 1700s. It was a farming community, a mill town under David Felt, a lonely group of deserted homes, and for a short time experienced renewed life as a summer resort. It's also been a late-night destination for bored teens looking for a scare, thus getting them involved in all sorts of mischief. This isn't a ghost town by any stretch of the imagination. Today, some of the buildings have been renovated for private use while others are awaiting proper attention.

The first settler in the vicinity was Peter Willcocks from Long Island. After damming Blue Brook he built a sawmill, selling the output to other settlers. Once the land was cleared, his family and descendants farmed the area for the next hundred or so years.

Enter David Felt in 1844. A manufacturer of stationery from New York City, he started buying land from the Willcocks family with the intention of building another paper factory to supply his store. (He already had one factory in Brooklyn.) From 1845 to 1847 he built the factory, put his own dam on Blue Brook to supply the power, and raised the town that housed his workers. His village became known as Feltville. Mr. Felt set himself up as an emperor of sorts, becoming known as King David. Residents were required to attend Sunday services at the big house up the trail, which doubled as the town store. The townspeople could buy produce he grew and meat from his livestock at the store and there was even a post office inside. A one-room schoolhouse stood up the road where the parking lot is today.

The first structure we come to is the Masker's Barn, an 1882 structure from the Glenside Park era, used to store carriages and horses that transported residents to the train station in Murray Hill. There is presently some renovation underway. Just up the road are three small Feltville homes that may have been used by childless couples working in the mill. Passing the third home, the road downhill goes to the mill ruin we walked by earlier today.

Staying on the main road, four more cottages in various states of disrepair come into view. The orange plastic fencing prevents us from close inspection and unfortunately, it gets in the way when we take our cameras out. There were four other buildings on this block, which have been either burned down or removed, for a total of three buildings in the front row and five in the back. By 1850, there was a total of about 175 people living in these buildings. All the buildings were divided in half by a common chimney and wall, with separate entrances and staircases in each section.

Continuing up the road, the store/church building comes into view. Resist the urge to check out the path to the cemetery. A small welcome center is on the ground floor of the big building and is open during the summer. The Adirondack porch and steeple were added to the building in the later Glenside Park years.

The little town survived Felt's rule until 1860, when it was sold to Amasa Foster. The former emperor then returned to New York City, possibly due to his brother Willard's poor health. Upon leaving his kingdom, Felt is reported to have said, "Well, King David is dead and the Village will go to hell!" The property changed hands six times over the next twenty years, with some businesses manufacturing cigars, silk, and sarsaparilla, but none were successful. By late 1880, the town was known as the Deserted Village. King David's prediction had come true.

Feltville was bought in 1882 by Warren Ackerman, who converted the property into a summer resort and renamed it Glenside Park. All the buildings were renovated and some, like the store/church, were given Adirondack accents. Dormers were added to the larger cottages to make the second floor more livable. The improvements gave each old building some new life and a unique personality.

Glenside Park offered its residents golf, croquet, tennis, baseball, fishing, and horseback riding until 1916, when times changed and the automobile allowed people to travel further into the country. Glenside Park, like Feltville, began to fade into a deserted village again. In 1920, the property joined the Watchung Reservation and the houses were again rented in the 1960s. While it's far from deserted, the Deserted Village is still a distinctive feature of the park and well worth a visit.

One more site to visit that's related to the village lies just ahead on the Sierra, and that is the historic cemetery on the hill behind the town. We can take the signed path up to the site. On close inspection, it seems there is a remarkable mystery here: John Willcocks has two tombstones next to each other. One is an original, but what's up with the new one? They're both for the same person, the son of original settler Peter. The newer tombstone is from an effort by the Daughters of the American Revolution to properly identify some residents of the cemetery who served in the military. None of these stones are standing on the actual grave site and it's possible there are up to twenty-four people buried here. It makes us uneasy thinking that we might be standing on someone.

Many footpaths spider-web away from the cemetery, but naturally it's the Sierra that we want. The trail continues along for 1.3 flat, muddy miles. Interstate noise occasionally intrudes as we pass by a

Feltville Cemetery

quarry, a Boy Scout campsite, and the dam for Lake Surprise. It's a fact that body parts were found floating in the lake during the early 1970s (and some more were found in a garbage bag fairly recently). The 1970s were a grim decade for this park.

When the Sierra crosses W. R. Tracy Drive at the end of Lake Surprise, we have some careful navigation to do. Following the Sierra around a wood fence, we'll bear to the right and then left as we follow a horse trail on a southeasterly bearing. The Watchung Stables and riding rings soon appear before us.

What is so interesting about some active stables? The buildings sit upon the launcher sites where the Army and National Guard operated Nike Ajax and Hercules missiles from 1957 to 1963. Nikes were the last of the ground-based antiaircraft defense systems. The control site (radar antennas and manned buildings) was located next to present-day Governor Livingston Regional High School, at the top of that closed road off Glenside Avenue that we passed earlier this morning. No trace of either Nike site is visible today but I'd be negligent in my responsibility if I allowed the historical significance of the place to be ignored. It's just another aspect of the deadly serious business we've come to expect from the Watchung Reservation.

The deadliest is quickly approaching. Following the entrance road for the stables brings us to Summit Lane, where we bear right for a few

Suicide Tower

yards before turning left on a foot path. We know what's coming up. A slight feeling of foreboding increases as we trek through the misty woods on our approach to the Suicide Tower.

Slowly revealed through the bare branches as we advance, the 150-foot-high water tower rises up before us like a giant tombstone, its top disappearing into the fog. Once we learn the structure's gruesome history, it becomes even more powerful and awesome.

There had been at least two suicides from the tower summit before the night of Tuesday, January 15, 1975. On that day, fifteen-year-old

Gregg Sanders, a sophomore at the private Pingry School in Hillside, came home from school at about 4:45 P.M. By most accounts he was a good student from a fine family and gave no indication to his teachers or school staff of any unusual home or school problems he might be having. Or maybe they just weren't paying enough attention.

Gregg was harboring a bleak secret that was about to come to light. The Mountainside Police told me he hadn't slept for a week, possibly fueled by the drugs that his sister, a nineteen-year-old college student in Massachusetts, had been mailing him. He had written a note to "Whom It Concern" prior to that day's event, and placed it under a paperweight on his desk. The note detailed exactly what was on his mind and what he intended to do.

His father, Thomas Sanders Jr., forty-eight, was an executive with First National City Bank. He was sitting at the kitchen table going over some bank paperwork when Gregg hit him several times in the back of the head with a two-foot axe. Gregg then struck his nightgown-clad mother, Janice, forty-four, once in the head when she came downstairs to see what all the noise was about.

Sanders then ran out of the house wearing only a T-shirt and khaki pants. Watchung Reservation was less than a mile from their home. The tall water tower at the eastern end was a popular spot after dark for youthful adults to see the lights of New York City or have some privacy. He headed to the water tower, climbed the cold steel stairs to the top, and then leaped out into the January night after slitting his left wrist.

Four young visitors looking for a late-night diversion discovered Gregg's body at about 11:15 P.M. Attempting to notify his parents later that night, police discovered their butchered bodies and the bloody axe when they entered an unlocked rear door of the home since there was no response to phone calls or knocking. The suicide note in the upstairs bedroom stated that Gregg murdered his parents because he did not want them to live with the knowledge that he had killed himself. He killed them as an act of love.

The true motivation for the crime remains a mystery, though there is some documentation that Gregg endured some teasing from his schoolmates because he wasn't as good a student as his older sister was. How is it possible that no one at Pingry School or even his doomed parents took note that he hadn't slept for so long? He obviously had been living with this intention for a period of time. Why didn't any of his close friends or schoolmates pick up on this? Did they keep it to themselves?

The tower steps were removed soon afterwards at the insistence of the local PTA. The Pingry School has relocated. Gregg's sister lives in Connecticut, last anyone heard. The story made the *New York Times* and national headlines. It rose to local myth and is still subject to much embellishment and retelling. While many of the stories about horrible midnight activities in Watchung Reservation may indeed be just stories, this one is an unsettling fact.

The image of that indifferent steel tower rising up from its high point like some monstrous cenotaph is hard to shake, and it stays with us even after we have left it and are back on the path. We all look back at it over our shoulders more than once. Heading back on the Sierra (by the trail, not the bridle path) toward the Nature and Science Center, we experience a dolorous feeling that will remain with us for a while after the hike is done.

We won't end things this way. There is one trick left up my damp sleeve. Returning to our cars outside the Nature Center, we'll drop our packs and go inside. Eventually, a new visitors' center will replace this old building but for now, let's head over to the "Feathers, Fur and Scales" exhibit. The light inside is subdued. Various species of the local fauna are represented in aggressive taxidermic poses behind protective glass in old-fashioned dark wooden cabinets. A taxidermy exhibit lovingly explains how the skins are prepared. Eagles and vultures, among other creatures with sharp teeth or talons, glare down at us from the display tops as if we were field mice ready for the kill. Down the hall, smaller avian species perch silently through the decades in their more peaceful dioramas. Thank heaven for the fluorescent rock exhibit.

Stepping back outside into the cold air, we reflect on this insane outing. The Magic Forest, Lake Surprise with its floating body parts, the Deserted Village, Suicide Tower, and some snarling, stuffed predators are all appropriate objectives for a long hike on a rainy day.

23
West Point Foundry

WHERE ※ Cold Spring, New York

WHY ※ Extensive foundry ruins

DIFFICULTY ※ Easy, a mile or two

MAP ※ None

WEB SITE ※ www.westpointfoundry.org

CONTACT ※ Foundry School Museum, 63 Chestnut Street, Cold Spring, NY 10516; 845-265-4010

DIRECTIONS ※ Taconic State Parkway to Route 301 West. Continue west on Main Street in Cold Spring (toward the Hudson River) and bear left on Marion Street/Furnace Street. Make your first right turn and wind down to Kemble Street, where you make a left. (Kemble Street, by the way, recalls Gouverneur Kemble, owner of the Foundry at its inception.) Continue down Kemble Street to the end, where you'll see a fenced-in area. Park here and walk further down (continuing in the same direction) through a fence opening and into a nature preserve.

This is a short trail that circles the remains of the once powerful West Point Foundry. After entering through the gate, bear left and walk along the shoreline for a few steps. Look to your left and find where the blue trail heads into the woods. Another side of the trail goes straight ahead; take the left-hand fork.

The foundry was built in the 1820s primarily for the construction of ordinance, but it also manufactured locomotives, engines, and

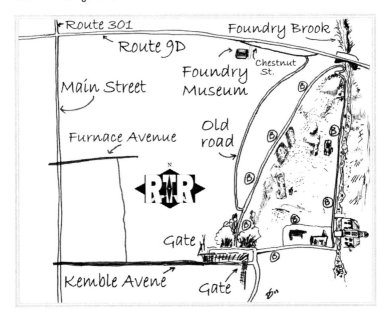

machine parts. During the Civil War years, West Point Foundry hit its peak. Foundry superintendent Robert Parrott had perfected a rifled cannon that was powerful, accurate, and was produced here. The supply couldn't keep up with the demand! The foundry used huge amounts of natural resources such as locally mined iron ore, water, and trees for the furnace. After the war, peacetime and the lack of demand for fresh cannon began the foundry's decline; by 1920 parts of the property were being leased to other companies. Nickel-cadmium batteries were produced as late as 1970. In later years, Foundry Cove was a Superfund federal cleanup site due to the massive amounts of heavy metal dumping that took place over the manufacturing years. Partnering with Michigan Tech, the environmental organization and land trust Scenic Hudson has been employing industrial archaeology students to clear and uncover the historic sites.

A good idea for this tour would be to plan our walk for when the Foundry School Museum is open (call for hours). Follow the blue trail to a point where a road comes in on your left (north). Leaving the blue trail for the moment, bear left and take the road (uphill) to where it meets Chestnut Street in Cold Spring. Follow Chestnut Street to the left and the museum will shortly be on your left. The Foundry School Museum has rotating exhibits on things Americana as well as lots of artifacts from the foundry. Let them know we're following the foundry trail. They have assorted historical books and pamphlets for

West Point Foundry wall

sale, and a knowledgeable staff. It's a pleasure to have a good museum near our ruins.

Return to the old road and follow it back to the blue trail. This time head left on the blue trail, which rings the manufacturing area below us and to the right. Follow the trail almost up to the Route 9D bridge, where the iron ore furnace remains have recently been excavated, and then back down along Furnace Brook. From here we can

West Point Foundry ruins

West Point Foundry office

clearly see the ruins and foundations of the manufacturing buildings. The furnace was at the top of the cove, below it was the blacksmith shop, and below that was the machine shop. Slag is everywhere. It looks like gray volcanic rock but is really light, porous waste from the iron-making process. We have to make sure we inspect the area carefully, because many features are not visible from the trail.

Finally we are getting closer to the main attraction of our quest: the Foundry office building. It's the most notable ruin down here and thankfully, it's in reasonably good condition. The office was erected in 1865, a time when the Civil War was over and the foundry was beginning to come upon hard times. The two-story structure stands in faded glory along Foundry Brook, awaiting renovation.

After exploring the office building, we'll poke around the other edifice shells nearby. Returning to the blue trail, follow it down to the beach, where it bears to the right and eventually heads back to where we began. As we're walking back, peer over your shoulder at the large and conspicuous white mansion perched on the hill. That would be the Hudson Valley's famous and occasionally abandoned Dick's Castle, currently enduring a conversion to new life as an apartment building.

Appendix

Places That Aren't Mentioned in This Book

For many reasons there are some very interesting places that are worth a look, but unfortunately, will not be endorsed for a visit. Some are closed to the public. Some are dangerous. Some have been altered in a way that changed the flavor of their former greatness. Some places just aren't big enough or don't have walks that are long enough to qualify as a hike. One has a lady that ticked me off.

CLAUSLAND MOUNTAIN NIKE BASE, NEW YORK

High above the town of Piermont sit former radar installations on Clausland Mountain and Mount Nebo. These Nike Hercules missile sites represent the last of our country's land-based antiaircraft shore defenses circa the mid-1950s. There are quite a few of these former Nike missile sites in the New York City area. Fort Tilden in the Rockaways comes to mind quickly and if you are lucky (or sneaky), you might be able to enter the underground rooms where the launchers and missiles were. Don't get too excited at this prospect since there is nothing there and the rooms are small.

The mountaintop site is now Clausland Mountain County Park. To reach it, take Route 9W south from the Tappan Zee Bridge. Heading in that direction, turn right (west) onto Route 28, Clausland Mountain Road, and then left (south) on Route 5, Tweed Boulevard. In another half mile or so, you'll see Nike Lane, so make the right turn and go all the way uphill (bearing to the right) to the parking area. Once at the parking lot, spend ten minutes of your time looking around at the water tower, utility poles, antenna platforms, power building, and scattered concrete pads that mark the spot where the old buildings were. An orange trail snakes through, heading toward the Long Path before looping back, but don't do that yet. Do the walk-through and return to your car.

Heading downhill, make the right turn and you'll see a trailhead and signboard. The blue trail proceeds downhill for a short loop to an overlook, while the orange bears uphill, intersecting with the Long Path in another loop (orange and the Long Path run together for a short while). The road continues through the gate to a caretaker's property. Continuing on, it climbs Mount Nebo and arrives at communications towers. Nothing else is there except for a few more building pads. If your intention is further exploration, the orange trail loop awaits you. Alternatively, you could hike from Tackamack Town Park on Clausland Mountain Road (see the Army Tunnels chapter) up to here and then retrace your steps back for a round trip of about 6 miles.

Nike Town Park (north and south parcels) was the site of the radar tracking equipment for the Nikes. One launch site was on Route 303, presently an Army Reserve center. I'm told all the missile rooms and machinery have been removed or filled in. The other launcher site was on Campgaw Mountain in Mahwah, New Jersey, also removed. Even though this site might be the textbook example of a "road to ruin," the scarcity of actual remains makes it impossible for me to include this location in the book.

THE ERIE CANAL, NEW YORK

I'd like to hike down the Erie Canal Towpath loudly singing "low bridge, everybody down" endlessly, because they're the only lyrics to the song I know beside "sixteen miles on the Erie Canal." The problem is that the good ruins are spread too far apart, making it hard to come up with a hike that makes sense. You'd have to *drive* to do the Erie Canal, and what fun is that?

ECKLEY MINERS' VILLAGE AND CENTRALIA, PENNSYLVANIA

Located 9 miles east of Hazleton, Pennsylvania, off Route 940, Eckley Miners' Village is a nineteenth-century "museum ghost town." It was once a coal mining company "patch town," where miners lived. Today it is a state park, good for an afternoon's exploration, but not really a hike. There are numerous miners' homes to explore as well as a church and other structures. Admission is charged.

While you're investigating Pennsylvania's ghost towns and coal heritage, check out Centralia. That's a ghost town in the truest sense.

There has been an underground coal mine fire burning there since the mid-sixties, resulting in evacuation of the townspeople. All that's left is a cleared town site (many buildings have been razed) and the constant smell of something burning.

FORT MONTGOMERY, NEW YORK

The new Twin Forts Trail, encompassing Revolutionary War Forts Clinton and Montgomery, begins at the Bear Mountain State Park zoo under the Bear Mountain Bridge and winds toward newly uncovered remains at Fort Montgomery. There are no real ruins at Fort Montgomery, just some cleared foundations and two fenced-off mine holes. You can pretend to aim the cannon that are placed at the historic batteries at the pleasure craft passing by on the Hudson River. Fort Clinton stood where the bridge is now, but an earthen redoubt in the zoo is all that's left.

You might pick up the Appalachian Trail in the Bear Mountain Inn parking lot, take it through the zoo, and then follow the trail into Fort Montgomery over the new suspension bridge. That's about a 3-mile round trip.

HARTSHORNE WOODS PARK
AND SANDY HOOK, NEW JERSEY

There are several World War II military remains at the former Highlands Army Air Defense site near Sandy Hook, New Jersey. There are a number of military leftovers at Sandy Hook, too. I tried to come up with an interesting hike in each of these parks and ran into problems.

Hartshorne is a large park and all the places we want to see are at the eastern end, off the Rocky Point parking lot. You could park at the Buttermilk Valley Trailhead on the other side of the park and do a 7-mile round-tripper to visit the military section, but if you do hike the Grand Tour trail, you'd be sharing it with bikes and horses. I don't even want to run into other people when I hike, let alone horses or bikers.

Beginning our hike, the RTR Investigation Team started at the east end and spent the better part of three hours wandering around the old military section. You could shave it to two hours or less if you stay out of the two fenced-off gun emplacements near the shoreline and the other solitary bunker that's on the Bunker Loop trail just past the Rocky Point parking area. The Command Loop is a high point with no artifacts. All of the walking in this section is on asphalt. People come here with their children and dogs.

Sandy Hook has many interesting military things to see. So much, in fact, it's better to do it by car. The lack of marked trails makes it challenging to stitch the better sites together on a hike that makes any sense. The other half of the problem is that some of the gun emplacements are only open during Park Service tours, which is a great way to go (www.nps.gov/gate/index.htm). The tours take you into some batteries you'd never find on your own. The rest of the time the sites are sealed tightly and not open for inspection, and no, you won't be able to sneak in.

JUNGLE HABITAT

The ruins of this former drive-through animal park are available for exploration near West Milford, New Jersey. To get there, follow the directions for Long Pond Ironworks in chapter 12 but continue about 2 miles farther west on Route 511 to the signed turnoff for a small airport. As you're heading to the airport, where you'll leave the car, you'll see the unmistakable entrance to the park on the left.

Warner Brothers ran Jungle Habitat for about four years during the mid-seventies. Cars getting damaged on the drive-through and reported mistreatment of the animals eventually led to the place's clos-

Jungle Habitat gate

ing down. The property was recently added to Norvin Green State Park, allowing legal exploration of the site.

From the airport, walk downhill to the big wood frame at the park entrance. After passing through the opening in the gate, it's a long uphill driveway walk to the massive 3,000-car parking lot, where you'll find twin tunnels that lead into the walk-through section.

The reason why I haven't added it to the book is that although it is lawful to enter, there is a confusing maze of unblazed paved trails that snake around both the walk-through and drive-through sections. I couldn't possibly lead you through in print, but if you have the time and a GPS it is a worthwhile place to visit. You can bike the drive-though part . . . if you can find it.

LENOIR PRESERVE AND UNTERMEYER PARK, NEW YORK

These two properties are almost next to each other in Yonkers. To get there, take the Saw Mill River Parkway to Executive Boulevard. Go up the hill and then bear left at Route 9. Untermeyer Park is 0.25 mile on the right, just past the hospital.

Samuel Untermeyer's mansion stood where the hospital is today, just north of the park. He built his garden, walled it off, and stuffed it full of Hudson River overlooks, reflecting pools, bridges, statuary, columns, cherubs, and paths that follow channeled water as it flows to nowhere in particular. The garden would be delightful if not for the rundown condition it is in today. Paint is peeling and cement is falling. The statues and tiled pools are chipping and weathering into nothing. Actually, this decayed condition is perfect for us ruin-hunters, but there are two compelling reasons not to include it in this collection of places to visit:

First, the sign outside the garden says, "No photography without a permit," and they enforce it. I didn't know about the sign the first time I went to investigate. There is a community center/office on the path before the entrance to the formal garden. I went inside to speak to a staff person about the history of the place and to possibly get a map or some printed information.

Her first words were, "Is that a professional camera?" She was eyeing my Pentax SLR.

"It could be, I suppose," I said.

"Are you a professional photographer?"

"Sometimes."

"You can't bring that camera into the garden."

I was stunned. She told me about the sign. I said I just wanted to look around and wasn't shooting professionally. (At the time, I was not working on this book.) She insisted that I needed a permit to enter the garden. I asked her if police were going to wrestle me to the ground and confiscate my film if I had the nerve to enter the garden without a permit but she repeated the signage warning. I said it was a pleasure visiting the park and left. I couldn't believe it! After all the off-limits places I've visited during my long career as an "urban explorer," I couldn't get in here with my camera. More determined than ever, I returned a week later *without* my sometimes professional camera, using my then four-year-old son as a "beard."

Second, the place is very small. Nicely decayed, loaded with endless photographic opportunities but still it is small and you can't take pictures without a hassle. There is a short trail heading past a strange domed rock sculpture. A path twists over and through the rocks. The trail, which leads down to the Croton Aqueduct, goes downhill through the woods, sometimes getting very overgrown and washed out. The people who run Untermeyer Park are hoping we don't recall that David Berkowitz lived in Yonkers and partied hearty in this park and some caves down along the aqueduct pathway with his Satanist friends before and during the Son of Sam murders in the summer of '77. The city of Yonkers has since sealed up the caves that those dark rituals took place in. The park has a historic significance that the city is trying to forget about to this day.

Lenoir Preserve is about a half mile north of Untermeyer, containing the remains of the Lenoir estate. Visit the nature center and follow the paved paths as they wind around the preserve. There is a gazebo, old stone walls, a castellated stone arch gate on a trail that also eventually winds down to the aqueduct, and remains of terraced gardens. Stone steps abound throughout the property. The old mansion is now used as a culinary school.

Items of interest to us, though, lie at the end of the main paved path as it heads in a southerly direction. Look for an open eagle-topped steel gate and then pass through into the wonderfully crestfallen ruins of another formal garden. This is much smaller than Untermeyer's but chock full of colonnades, cherubim posed on fountains, and a few reflecting pools. Damaged faces, full on and in profile, sorrowfully watch over the ruins while short paths just begging for exploration meander around the grounds. The big Alder Manor Gardens mansion, also suitably rundown, sits in faded eminence next to the garden. The place is under seemingly perpetual renovation.

Alder mansion garden

Alder mansion

NAVAL WEAPONS
INDUSTRIAL RESERVE PLANT

The old Grumman F-14 warplane facility closed down years ago, leaving the pine-filled eastern end of Long Island with some really big hangars to fill. Private industry has moved in to occupy the place, giving curious history hunters a chance to drive respectfully around the formerly top-secret base.

To get there, take the Long Island Expressway all the way out to exit 71, Calverton. Make a left at Edwards Avenue and follow it up to Route 25, where you will make a left turn (west). Just past the junction of Routes 25 and 25A is where the fun starts. Grumman Memorial Park sports an impressive bomb-laden F-14, which sits atop a concrete display. The East End Aircraft L.I. Corporation hopes to add a history center and museum to this park, and possibly more aircraft. Check out www.grummanpark.org for details and the chance to buy a brick on the Walk of Fame.

A control panel outside the guard booth in the park has two push buttons. Push one button and the lights on the tail and wing will come on and the other one energizes the landing lights underneath. I'm not sure why, but this is *so cool*!

Okay, enough gawking at the plane. Continue west on Route 25 (interesting control tower that you spotted across the field) and turn left (south) at Wading River Road, looking for the sign pointing to Manorville. In about a mile, turn left onto Grumman Road and pass by some old Northrop Grumman office buildings. Your "ruin sense" should start tingling right about now. Make a left down the road a bit into Calverton Enterprise Park.

First, pass by the unoccupied guard booth. There are some mighty big hangars around here to marvel at and auxiliary support structures are all over the place. Think about it, you're on an old top-secret research base. F-14s were tested here!

There are expansive, abandoned, weed-choked parking lots in front of some buildings. There is no set route to follow, just drive around and you can't help but wind up on one of the two massive old runways. Look around for "Aircraft Only" stenciled in white letters on the wide concrete strip. Careful exploration will put you onto the airfield near the blast fence, right by the control tower. One of the more remote vacant hangars has a tantalizing, partially open door up on the top floor.

Private businesses are housed in some of these structures and most likely they would not take kindly to strangers entering buildings without permission. The folks who run Grumman Memorial Park are not offering "inside" tours of the old proving grounds, but who knows what the future may hold?

NIKE BASES

There are a few old missile sites around (such as at Clausland Mountain Park), usually in parks with other military features. None can be entered without being on a formal tour (notably at Fort Tilden). Most sites in this area have been sealed up, although some in the Adirondacks are available for sale.

POTTERVILLE

Potterville was an honest-to-gosh ghost town sitting beneath mountains and along a stream in the Catskills. It was part of the Lundy (of Brooklyn restaurant fame) estate until recently, when the State of New York acquired the property. There used to be many buildings on the site to investigate, including barns, a school, homes, and bungalows. The old hamlet was vacant by the 1930s.

From the town of Wawarsing on Route 208, you had to find Lundy Road, turn north (you can only go one way), and then follow the road a few miles. The last mile in is on a four-wheel-drive road and unsuitable for most regular vehicles. There is an area opposite a gated property where you can park and then walk the last mile into Potterville.

Potterville

Many of the structures were in poor condition. Evidence of neglect and vandalism over the long years was obvious but the place was interesting to explore. I wouldn't go into most of the remaining buildings because the floors and roofs were rotted out, but the school was okay and the barns were likewise safe to enter. The feeling of the old community was still present.

Once the state took over, they razed all the buildings on the site. Too bad. I was lucky enough to visit twice in the last few years and photograph what was there. I understand that part of the Long Path hiking trail might soon be relocated through Potterville, but the old ghost town is now history in the truest sense.

REGAN POINT AND CAMP BLISS

This isn't a hike at all but an adventure of an entirely different sort. The spotty remains of a private miniature "Great Camp" can be reached by kayak or canoe if you drive up to the Adirondacks and head towards Little Tupper Lake, 7 miles west of Long Lake. Once at the lake, paddle a mile or so across to campsite #7 and marvel at the remains of the mini–Great Camp that used to be extant at Regan Point.

The entire vicinity is known as the William C. Whitney Area (518-624-6686), after the gentleman who owned it before the state took over. Whitney established "Great" Camp Bliss at the western end of the lake sometime around 1923. Nothing remains at the site but it is still a popular paddling destination.

A Mr. Regan was secretary to Mr. Whitney, and gained permission sometime in the 1920s or 1930s to build his own, much smaller version of a Great Camp at what is now called Regan Point. Two lonely fireplaces are attached to the ruins of what must have been fun buildings to party in. There are some stone pillars in the water as you approach. There might be more artifacts awaiting discovery if you poke around and look in the corners. The best part is you can camp there for free, overlooking the magnificent (motor-free) lake. At night, the ruins silhouette against the stars as the loons' otherworldly cries carry eerily across the water.

About the Author

David A. Steinberg is married, has a son, and lives in Westchester County, New York. Over many years he has planned and led hikes and tours for several different organizations. Using photography as an excuse, David continuously attempts to satisfy a long-time fascination with ruins, ghost towns, and similarly abandoned places.

Hiking the Road to Ruins features some of his favorite New York City–area destinations, collecting years of dedicated exploration into one volume.